THE PROPHETIC ARC

A Prophet's Backstory

I0559353

Ken Cox

REJOICE
Essential Publishing

Ken Cox/Rejoice Essential Publishing
PO BOX 512
Effingham, SC 29541
www.republishing.org

Unless otherwise indicated, scripture is taken from the King James Version.

The Prophetic Arc/Ken Cox

ISBN-13: 978-1-956775-99-0

TABLE OF CONTENTS

FOREWORD

As I read *"The Prophetic Arc: A Prophet's Backstory,"* I'm re-minded that Apostle Cox's objective is to see the people of God grow and fulfill their purpose and destiny.

Having your pad and Bible handy will allow you to look back over the years and better understand why certain things had to take place in your life and ministry to reach your God-given purpose, gifts, and assignments.

You will understand that the process of your trials and testing was all in the making. The Lord has called you for His purpose; He will perfect them.

When reading *"The Prophetic Arc: A Prophet's Backstory,"* you may ask yourself, where do I go from here? This book will help you break free from stagnation and procrastination as you emerge in a greater capacity of God's anointing to operate in His grace, love, and accuracy while spotlighting character and integrity. Be encouraged and SOAR!

— *Apostle Virginia M. Spencer*

INTRODUCTION

Have you ever found yourself, as a prophet, grappling with the desire to distance yourself from your past, particularly the less favorable aspects? The truth is that we all bear these burdens in some shape or form. We are, above all, human servants of the highest God. Let us not forget that we are His *Amos 3:7* servants, united in our shared experiences.

This book will help you understand the ups and downs of life and that we were always in God's plan, even when it looked different. The prophetic arc is the prophet's process of developing and living through an invaluable series of experiences while enduring divine training.

A prophet's backstory is about living through those times and understanding how to communicate with God to become His prophet of relevance and that is a process. The prophetic arc of living through those times is the practice that God has us involved in as we develop the life skills of His chosen prophets. Our backstories are critical and important to us as they tie us to our future.

We will explore this and my assignment is to help you develop an awareness and understanding of what you have been through that is clearly for your good.

I understand that it may look differently, but despite how it looks we need to use the eyes of understanding so we will be enlightened by God. Our backstories leave us so often with unanswered questions and mysteries about our lives as we reflect on different times.

There is a clear-cut reality: we had no choice in our backstories. God has chosen us to be His mouth pieces in this world, carrying a message of hope, change, and deliverance, while we encourage, uplift, and provide direction to others.

Our jobs are not easy, and our training must be continuous if we are going to allow God to take us from Glory to Glory. We must develop to be effective. Finally, this work is geared to all levels of the prophetic. Some prophets may project maturity but are still emerging.

So now, let's dig into the prophetic arc to see the backstory revealed within the following chapters. As I continue to walk in the realm of the prophetic, I have noticed real changes in my life with friends and family. This is my prophetic arc as my personal backstory is created.

I dedicate this book to all of you who have experienced the same and have struggled to understand your deposited experiences. We are called to execute and take dominion and be trusted by God. This is His process of dealing with us individually. Thank you in advance for reading, "*The Prophetic Arc: A Prophet's Back Story.*" I pray that God blesses you as He reveals to you.

CHAPTER 1

UNDERSTANDING PROPHETIC ARC

One term we hear a lot within the prophetic circles is process. We speak about the process as if it was something that is the same for everyone. The reality is it is not and while the process of developing prophets is still an invaluable series of experiences, we need to understand that the prophetic process is a vital part of the prophetic arc of a prophet.

The prophetic arc as a term is not spoken of daily in prophetic circles, but it is a daily and critical process. The prophetic arc is the evolving process of the prophet.

The journey and the development of that prophet are played out in that prophet's life, day after day. Prophet consider your experiences, the good and bad, were all for a purpose. The prophetic arc shapes you as your life experiences turn and twist in all areas.

The prophetic arc will help us to communicate and understand the phases of a prophet's life that are so often overlooked or reflected as bad luck, yes, even the devil. The prophetic arc is connected to the God-given assignment of any individual prophet. The prophetic arc is unique for each individual prophet.

We all should be familiar with the prophetic call phase or being called into the prophetic. When acted upon, this shapes the core message of that prophet. The process happens through a prophetic arc as it begins in the life of that prophet.

Within this phase, there will be numerous experiences that the prophet will undergo, so that the prophet will evolve from or be stuck in. This is where we will have numerous experiences placing us on a high or a low. We are being tested and prepared.

Dealing with the reality of being called into the prophetic can be overwhelming for some and not a big deal for others. We all are different and we react to different things in different ways.

Our experiences move us in different directions, as our callings move us to various positions and experiences. We must remember that God is the master orchestrator of life itself.

Our obedience is a factor as we start to move in the various angles of the prophetic arc that God allows us to move it. Some prophets will move to prophetic training and prophetic empowerment within the prophetic community spectrum. However, there is a hard reality in that we are often stuck in the prophetic call phase. Where are you at on this issue?

This is a serious issue to consider when we reflect on whether we have not been trained, or accepted the training God put before us. We may have called it something other than training.

How many of us have failed to understand the process of expanding our sphere of influence and are stuck in our lives?

We are stuck because the prophetic arc of our lives tells us we need to see this through. What have we not done, that we need or should have done? We must work on ourselves, prophet. Look at this example: We have not dealt with the initial issues of our calling, so now we find ourselves moving through the motions without any substance.

When we have never learned how to solve problems, how can we help others? We never got that deposited experience, so now we have nothing for others because our depth of relationship with God is lacking.

Prophet, when we need to see it through, and we don't, we hurt our own cause and we fall for traps traditionally set for prophets. Do we not see that the prophetic arc is for our preparation for what is ahead in our lives?

We are still in the being called phase. We are going through multiple issues in our lives and we attribute it to bad luck, the devil, and other people's issues. We become masters of the blame game and God is not glorified in our lives.

How many of us realize that God has us to practice to become what He ultimately is calling each of us to do as we become the type of prophets and seers He has anointed us to be?

Joseph, for example, is a process of seeing the prophetic arc in its process. Let's examine just a few aspects of his life and understand the process of the prophetic arc.

He is a seer and a different type of prophet. We see Joseph in a situation where he is a slave but very prosperous. He was in a tough situation, but he had options in his life. He worked for Potiphar, who had given him free reign over everything. He could do what he wanted and how he wanted, and yet he was a slave. His only restriction was Potiphar's wife.

Joseph is a slave, but his life contradicts who he is. Still, despite his situation, he is faithful in guarding over and maintaining what his master had. His conduct reflects *Luke 16:12*. He takes care of another man's property. Joseph is trusted to handle the matters of another man with respect.

God deals with His prophets as He prepares them for where they will go and work for Him. Let's be real: This is a low point in his life. This is the Lodebar season of his life. We will share this concept in *Chapter 3*.

Right now, let's look at us today. How many of us have seen far too many prophets come to sit in a ministry to look for a personal opportunity and lose focus on maintaining and growing in a work God has given to shield and protect them?

This was not Joseph. He was given a personal opportunity to develop because he was where God wanted him to be. The prophetic arc of his life had positioned him.

Notice that Joseph did not do as we often do. We will ridicule and belittle individuals we were connected to in the pre-learning prophetic phase. We do this because there is no prophetic arc in our lives that elevates us to a place where there is a glamor stage. All we see are just a few people.

The sad part is that many of the now generation prophets do not understand this and never develop here as the prophetic arc angle of their lives does not agree with their self-perspective.

The lack of knowledge, mentorship, and ability to receive sound advice kills the prophet's ability to learn in a learning environment and stunts prophetic growth.

This is why today, within the prophetic, we have so little to stagnated growth. When the prophetic arc of our prophetic development puts us in a Joseph situation, do we do as Joseph did and figure out a way to learn what God has us there for or do we run away? This is a fair question.

The prophetic arc of God puts us in situations that look like bad situations. This is prophetic training. The prophetic arc of Joseph's life has placed him in a hole. Then, he is sold as a slave. He is at this low point in life, but he gets the needed training and experience to deal with what is ahead of him.

Joseph has to give his best to survive in this hostile environment. Prophet when you learn this concept, you will appreciate what God has done for you and thank Him for what you have learned.

So many of us feel like we will give our best to God when we feel we are elevated. This is the wrong idea. This is why the prophetic arc exists to expose the prophet to giving their best daily, not for a specific season. When the prophet gives God their best, God does a work in their life to increase and magnify the prophet's best.

There has to be an arc within a prophet's life. Look at Joseph again. From the time he is introduced in scripture, he is up and down.

Things are good and then things are bad. This is the roller-coaster of a prophet's life: You move from one extreme to another.

While we often blame the devil for our ups and downs, we need to understand that this is the cycle of a prophet's life. Some of you may be down today, and your life is the opposite of the prophetic word you have received.

The reality is that your life is moving in ups and downs to alert you to the fact that you are valued by God because of your calling.

As a slave, Joseph's life was awesome. Here he is, the same Joseph who was left in a pit to die and is now sold into slavery as a piece of meat would be sold. He has overcome and proven himself and is living a good life. He is a steward who is counted on. Look at the experience. He gets as a prophetic steward. This is his backstory.

He had to run an operation at Potiphar's expense. Today's prophets get to practice and execute ministry at someone else's responsibility and expense. The problem so many of us have is that we want to run a ministry without any practice. I can laugh at this fact today, but I remember when it was a nightmare to understand this.

The prophetic arc introduces us to the reality of living a good life that will never stay the same. There will be change. Even within the so-called good life, there will be ups and downs. All of a sudden, Joseph's life shifts from being a steward to being a prisoner. The reality is that God is still in control.

Potiphar's wife, with her antics, has thrust him into a level of preparedness. He now learns how people can in life speak untruths about you and God still get the Glory, while you're in one of the lowest points of your life. Prophets, your ability to have thick skin is critical in this aspect. Learn the lessons God is teaching.

Joseph gives us the example that every time we have a problem that there is a purpose. He shows us that the arc of our mantle will test us in good and more often in bad times.

Can you imagine Joseph going from a valued steward to a convict? He has now lost his job. Here is the icing on the cake. You must understand this. Joseph has done everything right and he still lost his position. This is now his life.

Prophet, what happens to your character when you lose publicly? What about when you are called a false prophet or scandalized for the sack of Christ and many times for the prophetic in general?

Does your character match your life condition? Does your character match your prophetic arc only if you are being blessed? Prophet, the question is tough, but it is fair.

Prophet, when the prophetic arc of your life shifts, and God is calling you to handle it, will you complain? Will you still trust God when the status is changed from having security to now being a convict? Joseph did just that. How many of us were still singing praises to God, in the midst of winter, when our lights got cut out?

Prophet, maybe a better question is, what do you do when your life shifts and you have done everything right, but you still experience a public indignity or a great disappointment?

Joseph did as the prophetic arc of his life adjusted. Are you a prophet who has been through the thick and thin times of your life to answer the call of God?

He was not just called; he was chosen by God to go through this experience to build him as a prophet/seer and a steward. Can you see or imagine yourself going through this type of situation and trusting God when everything in your life looks opposite of who you are called to be?

The now generation prophet of today understands that the prophetic arc builds a prophet of God in a certain season. Have you ever wondered why some prophets become bitter and never better? Can you pass the test of the prophetic arc?

Now in prison, Joseph has every reason to change, but because of his deposited experience through the prophetic arc process, he still trusted God. Have you ever gone through things that were so unfair that one day, you realized that you were being tested in an experience that showed you no opportunity?

Today, you must realize that, as a prophet, most people that you meet will only see you as an opportunity or a gift. They will not see you as a person. Our society and today's culture have dictated that, and you, as a prophet, can't be offended when people only see you for what you do and not who you are.

You are a contradiction to people you meet and know and they seem the same way to you also. The prophetic arc will have you to develop in a season of contradiction. Why you ask?

As prophets, we are called to deal with contradictions in every sense of the word. This is why the prophetic arc is important to our lives. Let's be real: you can't imagine your life without the prophetic arc. Think right now of all the good and bad times of your life recently, as well as within the last few years.

Prophets, as you ponder my last question, here are three things you should always be aware of and depend on throughout the process of the prophetic arc.

1. God will always be with you. God was always with Joseph, even in the prison.

2. God will always show you mercy. Despite what God is allowing you to go through, He will always show you mercy. God gives new mercy daily.

3. God will always give you favor. God will send people to favor you like He did for Joseph as he now finds favor with the prison warden.

Prophet, you may ask the question why is the prophetic arc important? Always remember it is about development and growth. This is the divine opportunity of developing a deeper relationship with God.

This, in turn, creates a back story of revelations, dreams, and even trances for some prophets. In Chapter 2, I will discuss this, as it is important for us all as prophets.

Our prophetic arc redefines our communication with God. We see now how the backstory comes into the focus of our lives. Do you pray a lot when things are well versus when things are not so well? Let's look at your backstory.

We all know that challenges can test our faith and they also reaffirm who we are called to be. Our time of walking in the prophetic as a prophet of God helps us understand the prophetic arc and the backstory it creates in our lives.

The prophetic arc awakens us to our mandate and mantles. We need to understand that our mandate as prophets comes from the authority of God. We are tasked as prophets with specific assignments. The beauty of the prophetic arc is that it shows us our direct responsibility as prophets.

On the other hand, the prophetic arc awakens the prophet to their mantle. You know the authority, power, and anointing connected to your gifting as a prophet. This is why your mantle can be passed down to those who qualify for it.

Prophet, are you open to understanding that our walking with God writes a story of known and untold issues in our lives? That's what we refer to as a back story. Let's discuss how the prophetic arc and back story work together.

CHAPTER 2

WHY IS THERE A BACK STORY PROPHET?

Let me answer the question to the chapter name. There is always a back story to any prophetic arc that God executes upon your life. The reality is that your prophetic arc is tied to your back story.

The experiences of a back story made you into a prophetic vessel for God's use. The prophet reading this and wanting to improve their prophetic gift are totally obligated to embrace their back story.

When we think of back stories, we must focus on a time of testing in a prophet's life. We are in preparation and our character is developing. There is a reality that we will not always encounter the same exact issues, but we will and very well may have some similar issues.

Consider what your back story reminds you of and what it has cost you. You simply can't ignore your back story nor can you live there. Are you aware of what has made and molded you? Have you quit on yourself and God? Are you too sensitive to admit it to yourself?

We, as prophets, are always going through something, in some way or another. Prophets going through difficult issues involves a refining of the total prophet.

Moses was in the wilderness in *Exodus 2-4*. In *Hosea chapter 1-3,* Hosea endured adultery in his marriage. The persecution of Jeremiah was another classic example of having a back story to connect with the prophetic arc of his life.

I have been fortunate to work with prophets who have special backstories. As they share, I sometimes wonder how God allowed me not to go through this or that. The reality I share here is that as prophets share their backstories, it gives them a chance to heal and grow.

We can't overlook that this is the step to allow you to grow in intimacy with God. This is why prophets must have relationships so they can grow.

Today's generation of prophets needs fellowship among their peers. They can talk and share with each other who have had a similar back story under a community of like-type gifts.

The biblical prophets in the schools or companies of prophets lived together. All they had were each other. The back story of every prophet was important to that prophet. There is much to be said for going through something and having someone to understand.

Every prophet of God goes through some type of trials. This is simply necessary for the prophet. Keep this in mind: anyone can prophesy. Never forget that. Remember that a prophet of God has a consistent, accurate prophetic work that is used to bless others.

We must have a vehicle to connect us to growth. That is our back story as our prophetic arc shifts. This is work, and understanding the work is the key to growing, leading others, and blessing others in the world.

This is why you and I must mature in our gifting and progress. God has placed us in specific situations for our prophetic gifts, using his wisdom in our positioning.

So, with that being established, let me ask this question: Why is the back story of a prophet so important? Let me list some reasons why the back story and the prophet arc are so key to a prophet. Let's look at five key points.

The prophet's back story provides an understanding of the prophet's background. This includes their experiences and perspective over the years of that prophet's life. The back story has the real motivation of that prophet and how they view the world.

The back story gives the prophet the foundation as a messenger from God. It has established the prophet's creditability and authority.

The prophet's back story connects the prophet to the broader narrative of their history and the relationship of God on the same level. This is where we see that the prophetic arc has placed the prophet in their position by God and now the prophet gets understanding and needed work.

The back story of a prophet connects the prophet to the same issues that everyone else has only more severe. The back office shows the prophet as a human being with struggles and challenges, allowing them to establish a better connection with God.

Finally, the prophet's back story establishes God's sovereignty in that prophet's life. Many will never see that the prophet is an everyday person just gifted of and by God. This concept is so critical to development within the prophetic.

So know that our back stories are the key to us growing in gifting, maturity, and revelation. Prophet, if you want to increase your accuracy and walk stronger in the prophetic, do not underestimate the effect of your back story.

Prophet, please understand that you are given to the Body of Christ, the church, the community, or the nation(s) and must be prepared. Your personal situation is congruent with your character and relationship with God.

Can you imagine being a prophet in a small town where no one knows you? The reality is that you have an unknown prophetic ministry. Let's look at you as we look at Samuel.

Samuel transitioned from a young unknown prophet to a prophet to the nations. He developed along the way. Go back and reread *1st Samuel chapters 3 and 16* to have a good reference point of coming from nowhere to where he went.

The reality is that it was not overnight. It was a process. One of our biggest failures is our inability to covet and learn from our back story.

Could it be that we get so hung up because we are competitive and compare and contrast with each other? Maybe some of us are so spoiled that we are still immature despite the storms God has brought us through. Yes, imagine that. We still have more work to do on ourselves.

When we look at the prophetic arc of our lives, there is much to consider. We have to consider the following: Are we still devoted to God? Are we still passionate about His way, laws, and will? Prophet, if we are ever going to learn how to discern spiritual seasons and challenges, we need to learn from our back stories.

Looking at various prophets should help us individually get a feel for who we are. Elijah is a classic example. Look at his activity with Ahab in *1 Kings Chapter 18* and his mindset and mentality in *Chapter 19.*

As we look into his life, can you see how you spend time looking at yourself and your accomplishments? When you have a breakthrough, all of a sudden, the prophetic arc of your life shifts again, and now you have your world turned around.

In *Chapter 3,* I will discuss the prophetic arc when it seems stuck or when you feel you are in the Lodebar season. Prophet, our ability to be true to God can and will be tested, but we must stand strong as God shapes the spiritual climates around our lives.

The influence we yield as we come out of a Lodebar season is priceless. How many times have we overlooked the critical role a backstory plays in this very important fact? The back story is our connection to what we have done or experienced.

God sets the standard for the work the prophet must do along the journey. Isaiah's vision in the temple in Isaiah 6 is a powerful example. Can you consider yourself and what vision or experience stood out?

What is the back story in your life that has been so profound that you know it was an experience that launched you into the heart of the prophetic realm and you will never be the same?

My point is that the personal struggles and challenges in all of our back stories are the issues that often give us insight into a deeper meaning.

We have to be aware that we are called to minister to the hard issues. The reality is that the people are more concerned with our gifts than they are with us as a people and that is a reality.

God has given us the gift of a back story to help us understand things like compassion and empathy when we walk in our prophetic callings. Our backstories will influence our specific messages, revelations and how we conduct our business within and outside the Kingdom of God.

The prophetic arc connects the back story and gives it life, just like a replay of a movie. We must be open to it to grow. I am not saying live in your past, but know that you have one and learn from it, even the low points of your life.

Speaking of our past and low points, can you witness, to being a prophet who has been to Lodebar? Have you had a low point in your life?

Your humility and dependence will deepen when you acknowledge your mistakes as you now position yourself to submission and sensitivity to the Spirit of God.

Prophet, we will only learn when we are willing to cut the cord on our past errors, so for us to understand that the back story carries weight is an understatement.

We have the chance to grow from our back stories as we learn how to exercise the unique spiritual disciplines such as fasting, solitude, and even meditation. This is to heighten our spiritual growth for the prophetic ministry.

The reality of our low points are highlights that we are equipped to learn from. We must consider these things to appreciate our back story.

Let us now consider being in Lodebar as it is a back story process of every prophet in some form or fashion. Let's talk about why the prophetic arc has put you there.

CHAPTER 3

A PROPHET GOES TO LODEBAR

Prophet, now that you have read the previous chapters and we have talked about prophetic arc and the back story of a prophet. My goal is to marry them together and elevate you as the reader to understand why and how this affects us every day of our lives.

Do me a favor. If you have not read the previous chapters, please read them, as the rest of this book is based on those two chapters. The prophetic arc always creates a back story for the prophet.

As we have explored the back story, let us now look at a season every prophet will experience in some form or fashion. Make no mistake, you will experience this season; let's refer to it as being a prophet who goes to Lodebar by way of the prophetic arc.

The term Lodebar means being in hardship and isolation. Lodebar is a place like that and more. We can attach almost anything undesirable to describe this place. Oh, how the prophetic arc has positioned us in this kind of place. Read on and let's look at David.

Can you imagine being in a place where you feel time itself has been forgotten? You feel left out of the main stream of life. There is a gap between you and where you desire to be. Prophet, just understand that this is the place you're in.

This is not where you want to be, but it is where you are. Imagine the reality of being in a place where communication seems to be non-existent. Prophet, allow me to welcome you to Lodebar.

The economic and social prosperity and reality are dead in your life. Opportunity and blessings are nonexistent to you. The reality is that anyone in this position would want to be far away from this place. This is Lodebar, a place that thrives and yearns for those of you who are lacking. You are totally exposed and in need of relief. Is this you?

Lodebar is displayed as a definite part of your back story, as the prophetic arc has delivered you here. You need to learn about this place to be familiar with and understand its purpose in your life. Welcome to the place where no one hears you cry out but God.

Welcome to the place that seems like death with no sign of life. It's a place of no vegetation and no desire, either. This is the place the prophet comes to know well. A lot of us tend to forget it, so we move forth and ignore it. It's a small wonder. We never seem to understand the place known as our personal Lodebar.

I am driving this point home because many of today's prophets would rather forget our time in this place. We always want to walk tall, but let's not forget when we had to crawl and start. The times were so beneficial to us.

Prophet, what's important is that we understand that as physically depressing as the place sounds, it is worse in the sense that your life can mirror this, and mentally, you could go crazy trying to live in it and bring yourself out of it. Can you relate to this in your life prophet? The point is that you need God.

Let us start to focus here on a prophet and a king. Someone who God has handpicked, and the issue here is that there has been much controversy with the rise of David. Yes, please understand. I recognize David as a prophet who would become a king.

David shows us the real meaning of "determination of purpose." Determination of purpose works only for the prophet who knows they are walking in the purposes of God and what He can do.

There has been an attempt to kill David on top of everything he has been through but he went through the process of development. The process of prophetic development can only be accomplished in your life when you know God intimately.

David's life demonstrates a fact that prophets have experienced for years. The fact is that you are attacked because of the anointing on your life. The enemy does not waste resources or time on what is already his. The prophetic arc of his life has placed him here and he is learning a lesson on life.

Prophet, sure you will be attacked. The fact that you were attacked is a sure sign of your anointing. This holds true whether you understand it or not. The fact is you are called and appointed by God. Remember this as your status grows in the prophetic.

The enemy of God knows and sees God's plan for your life and chooses to cut you off from your prophetic growth before you realize who you really are. David is anointed to be king at age 15 and yet there is a time before he becomes king of Israel.

He is anointed before he is sent. Just like you are, he is anointed before his assignment is fully revealed to him. David, who has a prophetic anointing and has been anointed by Samuel as a king is still shoveling sheep manure in the field. David is called to the nations and spends time tending sheep. You would be wise to remember this.

Imagine being 15 and knowing and carrying the burden of leadership. Can you see why the prophet's mentality and their patience must marry each other?

This issue was that David was anointed at 15 but did not become known or noticed by anyone until 19 because of the battle with Goliath.

Notice the prophetic arc as it shifts in David's life. This is the back story of David that develops. We see that Goliath was the tool God used in David's life. Let's take accountability for our lives and see what tool God is using in our lives as we experience our personal Lodebar.

Yes, he was anointed, but David allowed God to position him, which allowed him to soar. Prophet, hear this: many of the things in our lives we pray for God to take away are the very things that God is using to elevate us.

Seek wisdom and wise counsel. *Isaiah 58:11* says if we allow, He will guide us constantly. Seek it prophet. It does not mean you're not anointed.

This is the way God works, especially with His prophets. The issue, the situation in your life may be your Goliath. You may not have had to shovel sheep manure, but your situation has made you think and wonder.

You have a global anointing and you live in a town surrounded by small minds and tiny to no visions. God puts us in these situations to develop us. The Lodebar experience helps you move to the next dimension as you are mentally prepared.

The movement through the portals of life helps us see that there will always be a Goliath bent and determined to establish a specific gateway in your life that God has orchestrated. God establishes it. The saga of Goliath for David establishes him now as a leader and starts the process of his ascension.

Now, prophets realize that as you labor, as you live and as you may even seek to understand why you're here, you should shout and thank God.

We live with a reality that tries to make sense of what God is doing. Prophet, this is about a relationship with God.

Here you are, prophet, anointed and trying to understand why the anointing comes in your life first and the prophetic positioning comes and follows year after year.

This is a real reality. This is also why we see that effective prophets become the best versions of themselves first before they attempt to help someone become a better version of themselves.

The adversity of our lives is what God will use to elevate us This is the essence of the Lodebar process. We must realize that without the adversity, there would be no growth. There would be no need for the prophetic gift to be activated.

Adversity has shown us a Lodebar in each of our lives. God has taken that adversity and positioned us as prophets and seers in places, for His purposes.

David, in the prophetic sense, has gone through this and he has lived to share it with someone else. This is what the prophetic arc does and the back story gives us the reflection. You must be aware of this and you must experience it in the sense that God gives it to you to allow you to become His prophet, seer, and apostle.

This is the prophetic journey experienced in the uniqueness of each of our lives. We all will deal with this within the prophetic. You're a prophet. Yes, you may know what it is like to be in a place that time has forgotten. Others may experience Lodebar through financial drought, family or personal job issues.

The lack of opportunity and solutions puts you in a place where giving up seems to be the most logical option. You are directly placed in a Lodebar type situation for a purpose. This is what developed patience in David's life.

Sure, he is anointed, but his patience positioned him to learn in every situation of his life. The pain of David's life has positioned him for every step of the way, as he knows how to handle the prosperity and notoriety that comes with his position. Do you understand the importance of the prophetic arc of your life placing you in this position?

Those of you who are prophets or prophetic people seek greatness in God, as you want to be His absolute servant. Take a real close notice of David's life. Greatness in God is a rollercoaster process. You better be ready.

You are up and you are down. The reality is that the process is ugly, greased with controversy, and intrigue, as we see multiple times how David's life is in danger and the haters he deals with seek to destroy him.

Saul wanted to kill him after he battled Goliath. Then Saul tracked him down in the mountains and wilderness in yet another attempt to kill him. Let us not forget that David had to live in caves and hid from Saul. Did I mention the 600 soldiers who wanted to stone David to death in the Ziglag incident? Can you handle this?

Let's not mention how his brothers felt about him after he was anointed to be king, and this was after the fact that his father, Jessie, did not originally call him to the house to see if he would be the next king as we see that David was not a biological son of Jessie. David was his stepson. Reference *Psalms 69:1-9* and *Psalms 51:5* for that issue.

This is the process of changing and learning in our lives. He is a man who is in Lodebar and his ability to trust God is seen as David demonstrates it in a significant manner. Every elevation in his life seems to be marked by some type of drama. Prophet, please take note of this. The elevation of suffering is real.

Look at David as he is anointed as a prophet, a priest and a King. Drama has a purpose and it seems to follow him. God's purpose is wrapped up in David's life as he pursues his calling. Welcome to Lodebar, as it feels like it will never go away.

Prophets, so many of us have made the mistake as we see the slick advertisements and TV programs. We have seen people flock to the gift and never realize that the person who has the gift has walked through a personal version of their own Lodebar. Let's be real. They have a backstory that has been seasoned by their prophetic arc.

Did you ever stop and consider that if there was no gift, there would be no notoriety? There would be no need for the personal development and clearly no need for the prophetic gift, especially in today's now generation. We have been given an opportunity that we can't afford to take for granted.

There is shame in the fact that a portion of the Body of Christ today does not believe in the prophet or the prophetic gift. We have given great credence to this, as we have felt we could duck our Lodebar and move straight to the stage of notoriety.

This type of thinking is not welcome in true prophetic development circles and must be eliminated from our ranks and thought processes. Let me say that again. It is not welcome, and yes, it cannot be a part of our thinking or development.

The mantle of a prophet of God is seen in their ability to help others because of what they have been through. The work of God utilizing the prophetic arc in our lives is absolutely priceless. David demonstrated this as he went to an actual physical place that the scripture calls Lodebar, an Old Testament ghetto. Let's look at David.

The back story of being in a position to help others is illustrated as we see David's life was changed by a young man named Mephibosheth. In *2 Samuel 9,* we see the classic story of David, now king, seeking someone who may be alive from the house of Saul.

David finds the grandson of Saul and the son of Jonathan. He is lame. He is the exponent of what Lodebar and the life of a prophet are about.

He is Saul's only living relative. We now see David's true character and what he went through. David demonstrates that you really do have to have patience to be anointed.

The mere fact that he searched for Saul's relatives after what he went through with Saul shows who David had become. Patience always works through the anointing.

David spoke to Saul's servant Ziba and sought to know if Saul had any children still alive because they were all being killed. Look closely at what we see demonstrated in David's life as the prophetic arc has swung him into another situation.

Mephibosheth would have probably been killed also had he not been lame. As a lame grandson of Saul, he is not considered a threat to anyone. David, who has been in a similar situation, knows what it is like to be the odd one. He knows what it is like to be an outsider within his own family. Remember, David is Jessie's stepson.

The blessing he gave to Mephibosheth is priceless. He restores him and gives him a place to eat and fellowship at his table. He has done the job of a prophet as he has improved Mephibosheth's life. Think of where David started and the position he found himself in. Also, look at the lessons he has learned.

Can you see *Psalms 119:71*? It was good for me to be afflicted so I could learn the ways of God. Can you see this in your life? Can you see this in David's life? Can you see this in Mephibosheth's life, son of Jonathan, grandson of Saul? God hid him and it was good so that he may live and learn.

Everything and everyone who had been connected to Saul, even the sons of his concubines were killed, but the affliction of this grandson kept him alive. Now look again at David, who also should have been dead, but his personal afflictions kept him alive.

We have so many lost prophets today because of our unique ability to hide, duck, and dodge our afflictions. As we grow older, there are some things we just don't do, or better yet, won't do. This is how and where we become genuine lost prophets. We will discuss this in Chapter 4.

Prophet, please understand that you are still here for a reason. You are in Lodebar, or you're on your way. The secret is to have a determination of purpose and know that you're coming out of Lodebar. This is what makes us. This is what defines us. This is why we are able to do what we do.

The hard cold reality is that we do get lost and we must deal with what it means to be a lost prophet. Let's explore that now.

CHAPTER 4

WHEN A PROPHET IS LOST

A prophet in Lodebar has taken us to a place where we simply don't know ourselves. Can you imagine that your backstory has a chapter of your life where you are lost? My friend, the power of the prophetic arc is real and we seek to find ourselves when we know we are lost.

The very figure of a prophet is a beacon of divine insight and guidance, and that does not just happen in our lives. Yes, our paths as prophets are loaded with challenges, especially for those who find themselves lost within the experience of their personal prophetic arc.

Let's define what it means to be a lost prophet. This is a unique mixture of a struggle to comprehend and convey divine messages but also the personal turmoil of navigating this daunting spiritual landscape. Welcome to the ongoing process of prophetic development.

The journey of a lost prophet generally has various phases, such as a revelation phase. This is the initial divine encounter where the prophet receives a message or vision. Revelations can be cryptic, symbolic, or overwhelming in intensity.

For a prophet, interpreting these divine messages accurately is paramount. However, the ambiguity inherent in many revelations can lead to confusion and doubt. A prophet may question the validity of their visions or their own ability to understand them, creating a sense of loss.

Then there is the struggle phase. Here is where our personal and external conflicts prosper in our lives. We yearn to solve them, much less to understand and communicate their message.

Prophets often face skepticism, hostility, and persecution from their contemporaries. This external opposition can impede their mission, leading to a feeling of isolation and helplessness.

The fear of being ostracized or harmed for their beliefs can make it difficult for a prophet to maintain their resolve. Prophet, is this your story?

Finally, we have a fulfillment phase. The divine realization or manifestation of the prophetic word is often accompanied by significant change or enlightenment. This is a journey, to put it mildly. The prophet's personal transformation required to embrace a prophetic role can be extremely challenging.

We must deal with this prophet. We must reconcile their human flaws and fears with their divine mission. This internal conflict can cause a prophet to waver in faith and direction, contributing to their sense of being lost.

The journey of a lost prophet is a testament to the resilience of the human spirit in the face of divine expectation. It underscores the profound challenges and internal battles that prophets must endure to fulfill their destinies.

The prophetic arc is not merely a path of divine revelation but a crucible that shapes and refines the prophet's soul, transforming it into a true vessel of higher wisdom and purpose. Through their struggles and eventual triumphs, lost prophets illuminate the enduring power of faith and perseverance.

What happens when you're in the struggles of life and there is no point of reference? You're a prophet and struggle to identify whether your life has a foundation.

Sure, you're anointed and gifted, but what happens when you're struggling? You want to go to the next level and more than anything, but you are certain you're lost. The key when you are lost is to find God. While we should know this, let's look deeper.

Most of us need to understand the journey to appreciate all we have had to go through to find God. Answer these questions. If I told you that you may want to consider changing your mind on some issues, would you?

If I told you that you're lost in an environment conducive to your growth, would you believe me? If I told you God was waiting on you to sacrifice to reveal something to you, would you believe me? Whether you do or not is up to you.

For the sake of discussion, let's look at Samuel's life. As a young boy, he struggled under the tutelage of another prophet and priest, Eli. We can see some incredible revelations in Samuel's life. The prophetic arc of his life is in full force as he is in God's divine.

In *1 Samuel 3:1-7,* the child Samuel ministered unto the Lord before Eli. What's interesting is that he does not know God. The word of the Lord was precious in those days. Eli was a prophet on prophetic block, so there was no open vision and revelation from God.

So now we know that Eli is on prophetic block and God still uses him. Appreciate this fact when you are in a difficult situation with difficult stubborn people and you wonder why.

Look at Samuel as a little boy around Eli, a gifted, anointed and stubborn man of God. How do you think Samuel felt? The same way many of us feel.

One night, Eli and Samuel fell asleep and scripture says that the word of God came to Samuel in the temple of the Lord. Think about this as the Lord called Samuel: and he answered, here am I, but he ran to Eli.

Eli is his reference point and that is all he knows at this point in his life. We can say that he is lost because he is. He is lost at a whole new level now.

Samuel said, "Here am I, for thou called me." Eli says he did not call him. This happened a total of 3 times. The point here is to evaluate the issue of a lost young prophet. This is our life at this stage. We all are lost at some point.

Eli now recognizes the issue. Notice that he is on prophetic block but knows what is happening with Samuel. This fact alone is why prophets need mentorship and direction. Samuel simply did not know God and his opportunity was before him in one of the strangest and darkest times of his life.

We previously discussed why Samuel and any prophet had to go through this process. The struggle elevates you in wisdom and knowledge. Samuel, a prophet called to the nations, is in his initial tests. This is a topic I will expound on in Chapter 6.

Now again, we see that Samuel was very young. He had no relationship with God. The word of God had not yet been revealed to him. He is a lost prophet at this very moment.

Samuel's life is the perfect example of a lost prophet. Samuel is deeply affected by his lineage. Look at how his mother, Hannah, was lost in her ability and confidence to produce children. Having children was a badge of glory for the woman and her rival, Peninnah.

She is a woman who has lost her identity as a woman and she is desperate. She turns to God and makes Him a promise. Do you ever find it funny that so often it takes us to be desperate to seek God when we are lost?

Hannah is just like so many prophets today; our backs have to be against a wall, and then we will seek God because we are desperate. Hannah turns him over to Eli, after he has socialized. Samuel's birth represented a prearranged covenant. He is put in a system that is foreign to him and he is lost.

Samuel is in an imperfect system now. This is what the prophetic arc can and will do with your life. Prophet, reread this if you have to, but it is too important for us to ignore.

Why is it imperfect? Because there is no revelation. His mentor is on prophetic block, operating in a system that he has never operated in before, and he, for all intents and purposes, is lost.

Understand the fact that he is a young boy. He is away from his parents and with someone who is as lost as he is. Eli had the experience that Samuel needed.

Read this carefully about Samuel. To make matters worse, to demonstrate this, as we see him in a learning system, he does not know. In *1 Samuel 3:7*, he does not know God, nor does he have the word of the Lord within him.

Let me stress this again: He is Lost. Have you ever considered that we are operating in a system, gifted of God and yet do not know or understand His ways?

Why would God do this to this young man? God had a plan for his life. *Jeremiah 29:11* tells us that oh so clearly.

Please picture a young man, gifted, anointed, and lost. He is following the instructions of a man assigned to mentor him, and for all intents and purposes, this man, Eli, is operating on a platform that has him on prophetic block. Yet God has placed him in an imperfect system so that he can learn how to follow God.

Does that sound like us? Speak to yourself and declare and decree that you will trust God, though you're in an imperfect system.

Let me take this opportunity to welcome you to the prophetic and help you understand that you're trained and raised to work in flawed environments and systems so God can use you in these systems for His purposes.

Eli has two sons whom he did not handle properly, and yet God has assigned him to raise a Prophet to the Nations. What's funny is that God will grow, groom, and mentor you. At the same time, you are lost, along with chaos, drama, evil, pettiness, and even foolishness, to prepare you for nations that operate in all of the aforementioned and even more.

God can raise you in a dysfunctional environment and still reveal Himself to you and use you right where you are. Ask Samuel about that and see what he says.

I submit to every prophet, seer, apostle, watchman, prophetess or prophetically gifted person, you are in an imperfect world with imperfect people and God still intends for you to do what He has called you to do.

The next time you hear a prophet say they can't grow here or there, examine to see if they really have a gift. You can grow in darkness. I share this in Chapter 11. Prophet, you can grow anywhere, anytime, and anyplace that God would have you grow. Samuel did; now, why can't you?

We have to stop using the excuse that this place is not that or that this ministry can't teach us anything. Every ministry can teach you something, even if it is what not to do. You can learn that. The reality is that every ministry of God can teach you something. You must be willing to become a student.

They may not teach you the nuts and bolts of your special gift, but you will not tell me that God just put you there and all He did was waste your time.

Stop kidding yourself, your peers, and most of all, God. Leaders, it's time to find out who the prophets of this generation are versus who the prima donnas are.

Samuel learned about the house of God before he learned about God. Samuel is taught how to honor and appreciate the system of God before he meets and knows God.

Far too often, we want to go straight to the nations. We fail to learn how to travel, what our basic needs are, where we are going, and who is responsible for our stay. What are we going to do when we get there? Yes, multiple issues need to be attended to before we go before God's people.

You may want to minister to thousands of people at a time, but may have issues praying over your meal at the dinner table. Your ears are itching so hard to be accepted and recognized that you are not willing to be of use to God in your current situation because your ego has to be fed first.

To the competitive prophets, especially you sneaky behind-the-back, secretly competitive prophets, the reality is you're lost in a system where all you think you must do is memorize the word of God, and shout before His people. Yet, in the system, you fail to realize that you must know God for His word to become real. Say, ouch, prophet.

Samuel finds God in a situation that does not fit his understanding. He goes to Eli because he is familiar with him. He is not familiar with God. Eli's purpose, even as a leader on prophetic block, is to steer Samuel to his destiny. Samuel had a choice and he made it. He went from being lost to being found.

Stop being a lost prophet. The lost prophet is always looking for something wrong in others. You fail so miserably when you fail to see your faults and what's wrong with your ministry, your work for God, and what's wrong with the status of your calling.

I know by now that some of you may not like the prophetic arc or the back story that is created. While that is your personal issue, you are still indebted to God.

Stop being a subject matter expert on your friends' and peers' ministries. Focus on what God has called you to do. You're lost in this imperfect world system and you don't know it.

Finding God will give you purpose, focus, and direction. You will benefit from wisdom. *Isaiah 58:11 says, "The Lord will guide you continually."*

Let's look at his life and see what he is up against. He is a young man who is lost in a system and learning piece by piece. He is not beyond making mistakes. He has choices to make and his ability to fulfill his destiny depends on his choices.

He is serving and he does not know God! He is the heir apparent to Eli. He is the next prophet called to the nations, but does not know God. Like so many prophets of our generation, gifted and anointed but still lost.

Like so many of us, you're in the daily cycle of your local society and culture. You're like Samuel as you talk about all your duties and responsibilities.

You are serving and lost because you don't know the God of the system you have emerged in. This is why the prophetic arc is critical to understanding.

When you are marked for God, you have a destiny and when you find God, you find yourself. Do not overlook the fact that Samuel was a child, a little boy, disturbed, troubled, and left by his mom with a man he does not know. He is being told what, when, and how.

He sounds like a young prophet dealing with life on a stage that they are very uncomfortable with because he is lost. Think about that for a moment. Has life affected you in such a manner?

He has all the reasons in the world to turn away from God. Some of us probably would have turned from God if we were in a similar position as Samuel.

He struggled to discover who he was and what he wanted to become. Therefore, he had to find God. This is why he is a lost prophet. I am talking about a process within a system.

Look at the prophet. His struggle nictitates how we may or may not react. You may be a lost prophet or you may know one. A lost prophet takes on several traits. They can be jealous. A lost prophet is a prophetic predator, always trying to esteem themselves.

You see them on social media like Facebook all the time trying to convince people, in cyberspace and the world to include the body of Christ, how deep they are. They are the only ones seeing into the future.

This type of lost prophet will lie in a heartbeat, stab you in the back, and sell you out because all they really want to do is to get their name out there at your expense.

They will not work like Samuel. They would have destroyed Eli and had his blood upon their hands and operated like a Cain-type prophet, and told God they didn't know Eli rather than do the work needed to grow.

This prophet is lost; frankly, they are the most dangerous type of prophet you will ever meet. They do not know who they are and are unwilling to trust God or His appointed leaders for clarity. Their back story will always be filled with lies and deception. They have an image to keep up.

They run from leader to leader, causing trouble and creating drama, all under the name of Jesus. They claim a set of values they have never learned.

This is why they will not tithe, and if they do, it will be sporadic and inconsistent. They give an offering and the world knows it. When you ask them to be a prayer partner and your prayer request to stand in agreement is now part of their sermon or posted on social media.

They use social media to throw off on others, attack them, and justify it because they believe they have been wronged. Do you know this prophet?

Some people refer to them as "false prophets" because, in the zeal of their gift, they will steer you away from God. The lost prophet does not know or understand that all things work together for the good of those who love God *(Romans 8:28)*.

This is foreign to them as everything they do will drive you away from God to a spoiled spiritual child who refuses to grow because they are lost.

God had a blueprint for Samuel's success. Without God, Samuel would have been a talented failure, who was anointed but lost. According to *Jeremiah 29:11,* God has a blueprint for you. He knows

His plans for your life. Whatever area in your life are you lost in? I encourage you to find God.

Again, please understand that you are in an imperfect world and system. What would you say if I told you that your prophetic arc has placed you in a system of contradictions right now?

We live in a world of contradictory truths. We must discuss the ability to live in an imperfect system with multiple truths.

Remember, prophet the next time you put your mouth on someone, check yourself to see if the area you're talking about in that person's life is not in yours. See if you're lost in that area yourself or maybe you are contradicting yourself.

CHAPTER 5

THE PROPHET LIVING WITH CONTRADICTIONS

The previous chapters discussed some truths about the prophetic arc and a prophet's back story. There is also a truth we seem to so seldom consider. The truth about a contradiction is that it is always opposed to something else. The issue with a contradiction is that it can be true. Now, you can have multiple truths that contradict one another.

This can be a statement, lifestyle, situation, or idea. When a prophet lives with a contradiction, the reality is that the prophet learns how to live with multiple truths. Look at Moses and understand.

Numbers 12 shows something we see so often demonstrated in the Body of Christ: Separate truths that are opposite of each other. God has allowed your life to shift into a season of multiple truths and you must grasp the experience.

The prophetic arc of your life has positioned you. You must also understand whose truth you will follow. In *Numbers 12*, we see that Aaron, the older brother of Moses and Miriam, and his older sister spoke contradictions concerning Moses, their younger brother.

Prophet, you should thank God for your family. You have learned something priceless from them. You may know it or not, but it is a vital part of your back story. Let's see where the prophetic arc has placed you. Look and learn from Moses now.

They challenged Moses's authority, asking each other, "Has God only spoken to him?" Also, Miriam spoke against his wife because she was different.

The truth is that all three were prophets and God spoke to each of them, but Moses was the one God had given authority to lead. There is a reality here that can't be denied.

Think about this. Where did Moses come from? He was already in a leadership position when he was at the palace. The back story of his life has him in a leadership position before he left the palace.

Now, he has been in the woods for 40 years, but his past has trained him. God did it with the prophetic arc on the life of Moses.

There is the truth of one thing in your life and the truth of another thing that is totally opposite. Both entities are true, yet they are opposite from each other. Every prophet will experience this as they grow in their gifting. The ability to grow in living with contradictions will be necessary in ministering to people of different cultures, races, and backgrounds.

Many of you have been called upon to speak the truth of God's word, yet you find opposition, as some of you have been persecuted and others have had to deal with contradicting issues.

Some of you reading this already know that your prophetic arc has turned your life into a similar situation. God has called you to go to the nations, and you must understand contradictions to be effective in your calling.

Have you ever considered that you are in an atmosphere that will present multiple contradictions so that you can understand the moment you're in and that is preparing you to be used of God?

Dealing with the challenge of different truths and being effective in who you are is a skill developed through the trails of life. You will be able to stand when others may simply give up or run away from the challenge.

Everything that makes you the prophet or a seer is built on the fact that you are the product of your ability to deal with and live with contradictions in your life. As you look and self-evaluate yourself, consider this.

When you cannot live with contradictions, you will never understand who you are and what you are called to do. The reason is simple. The value of your life will not be based on your relationship with God. It will be based on the opinions, thoughts, and perceptions of those around you. That is a grave mistake.

We all know someone who has spent years trying to understand exactly what they have been called to do and has spent an equal amount of time dealing with contradictions in a nonproductive way.

We all know someone to whom this applies, even if it is the one you see when you look in a mirror. Prophet, you must also consider yourself.

Abraham is known as the first prophet. God called him His prophet and while the honor was upon him, he surely had many contradictions. Those who knew Abraham could testify to his dealing with contradictions.

One classic contradiction in his life is the king's desire to sleep with his wife, Sarah. Abraham was so scared and intimidated by this that he said Sarah was his sister and not his wife.

He is caught between the powerful king who lusts after his wife and two real life issues that contradict each other at his expense. This is the great irony of contradictions in one's life. There are multiple truths here. Yet, as a prophet, Abraham must learn how to deal with and navigate through the contradictions in his life.

Then, there is Zacchaeus, a son of Abraham, who lived with contradictions. In *Luke 19,* he had a position of power. He is known. Yet, he is short in stature. Imagine a short man with power in the biblical days?

Understand that Zacchaeus presented himself to Jesus. This was the favor he needed in his life, which is what many of us in the prophetic will not do or simply refuse to do.

We can always look at why we do not do what we need to do. Many of us find ourselves in places we have merited by our ability to deal with contradictions.

The reality of Jesus giving Zacchaeus the blessing of sonship from Abraham was priceless. What do you need from God that your pride contradicts?

Consider the fact that you're a prophet and people do not know you other than the fact that you're gifted in the prophetic. They see you but they know you only by the gift. They do not know the person. Again, all they know is your gift.

This is why they present themselves to you only in reference to your gift and they often contradict themselves to constantly steer your gifting in their favor.

Prophet, can you now understand that you will always be a false prophet to some people because you did not give them a good word, according to them?

Some people will be mad at you because you gave someone else a good word that they felt did not deserve it. Prophet, be prepared to deal with these types of contradictions.

These are the same ones who will contradict your status to the Body of Christ and the world. They have no regret as they smear your name, reputation, and relevance. They will have no reservations about it. This is what living with contradictions is all about.

Every prophet of relevance will deal with multiple contradictions in their life. Your prophetic arc has been steered in this direction for you to learn. Prophet, learn this valuable lesson.

This is why when people strive to take away your humanity, understand that they are not in your covenant circle. They are only in your life to demonstrate a principle you must learn. Your ability to deal with the contradiction is what will elevate you.

Today, prophets spend so much time trying to impress or dealing with the fact that we need to prove to people that we are anointed. This proves our inability to mature in our gifts as we grow as people.

What I am saying is that the inner man reflects the outer man. The prophet who learns the importance of developing the inner man will learn how to live with contradictions. This is why your back story will mean so much to you and you will cherish it.

Prophets, if Jesus became flesh to show us how to live with contradictions, we are missing the point when we feel we don't have to deal with them either. We accept that contradictions are not of God and that we should go the other way.

Contradictions of multiple truths have come to you to help develop you. They mature you and give you that deposited experience that only a contradiction can bring. God is the master orchestrator of life, so look how He guides us.

Let's consider that Jesus experienced many of the same things that we do, like temptation, betrayal, and contradictory things. Let us consider how Jesus handled them. This is the lesson we must know and understand as the now generation prophets.

Jesus knew who Judas was. Every prophet should know their prophetic Judas. Only a real relationship with God will reveal this level of discernment.

Betrayal in one's life is a lesson every prophet of relevance will know and experience. The contradictions can't hide themselves. Notice in *Luke 22 15-16* that during the Passover meal, when Jesus passed the bread, He was actually feeding his Judas. What's the point here?

The point is that Jesus did not block him on Facebook, delete his posts, or stop speaking to him because he knew who he was. Judas was a contradiction to everything Jesus stood for and yet we see how Jesus treated him. Jesus fed him and advised us to do good to those who would despitefully use us.

Matthew 5:44 is a key that many of us need to work on. Love your enemies and pray for them. Look at *Exodus 23:4-5* and see how we are to deal with the property of an enemy. How many of us need prayer in this area? I would not be stretching it if we say we all do. Let us learn from this principle of life.

Jesus did it so smoothly and today, we all, as prophets, struggle with the fact that many times, people want to contradict us or make us mad. They want to bring out that part of us that they feel will discredit us or make us contrary to God's will.

Think about yourself. Have you or anyone you know moved away from someone because of contradictions? Prophet, look at this and know there are two sides to this.

There is the side of you moving away, where people reject you because of your stand or your assignment. Then, there is the other side. It's the side of you that takes a stance to please or connect with a group of people, like your peers, distractors, or even your haters.

This is why prophets lose themselves. We go through this process as we deal with contradicting issues. Prophet, this is a vital element to prophetic development. Thank God for your prophetic arc.

Can you understand why training is important. The scripture says to train up a child and they may depart from the teaching, but they will return. When we do not train, we do not learn.

This is simply at all levels and in the prophetic, it is critical. Training stabilizes us. It helps you see the contradictions in your life and guides you on how to deal with them.

Prophetic training is what employs us for greater works. It takes our development to learn that we always have a reference point. Our human factor is connected to the divine presence of God. This takes practice over and over for our now generation prophets.

We need the work to be prepared as the prophetic arc shifts as God uses it in our lives again to prepare us. Constant work helps us become Godly qualified for the assignment of God. What I am saying is that we will be tested along the way and unless we pass the initial test, we will keep taking the same test.

The prophetic arc will continue to work on this area in our lives. Do you ever wonder why we seem to deal with the same issues repeatedly? It is because we have not passed the initial test.

Keep reading as you reflect on passing the initial test as the prophetic arc swings our lives into such a season. Do you remember your initial tests prophet? You accepted your call. You went forth and what happened? Let's discuss the initial tests.

CHAPTER 6

FORGETTING THAT WHICH IS BEHIND, THE INITIAL TEST OF THE PROPHET

Prophet, please take time to understand this chapter, as it will help you greatly. Your prophetic arc is closely tied to your initial test. Initial tests are also referred to as tests that you must pass to be held in consideration as a true prophet of God.

To help you better understand, let me point out some key points about your prophetic arc and initial tests. Let's create a back story for training.

A prophet's initial tests serve as a filter to validate their divine calling. The ability to pass the initial test is crucial for establishing the prophet's credibility and authority. Do you agree?

Keep this in mind when we speak about initial tests. The process is ongoing throughout the prophet's prophetic arc. The process of development is at work.

Your prophetic utterance is remembered as your back story, which people will speak of and validate you as a creditable prophet. This is why a relationship with God is critical.

In the previous chapter, we discussed contradictions. While we explored the issue, we need to see if the prophet's utterances and teachings align with scriptures and won't contradict them. This ensures the prophet's message is consistent with God's revealed truth, which is essential for their prophetic arc to be accepted.

The prophet's personal character, motivations, and obedience to God are also examined within their initial tests. A true prophet should glorify God, point out sin, and exhibit Christ-like qualities throughout their prophetic journey.

Passing the initial tests establishes the prophet's divine mandate and lays the foundation for their prophetic arc to unfold and be revealed to them. Their subsequent visions, teachings, and impact on the community will stem from a validated prophetic calling. Remember this prophet as you seek to establish your mandate and your mantle.

So when prophets speak of our initial prophetic tests, understand they serve as a gatekeeper, ensuring only that you become the prophet of God, as you embark on an authentic prophetic assignment. We can see that the prophetic arc carries the very seed of God's authority and aligns with His will for our lives as prophets.

Think for a minute prophet. How we respond to life's situations, whether pleasant or painful, reflects who we are. As a prophet, your response will expose your true spiritual condition.

Our response reveals our beliefs, values, priorities, and spiritual condition and focus on any particular moment because of who we are: Prophets of God.

In *1 Peter 1:7,* Peter, who I clearly see as a special but different type of prophet, calls the trials of life as "the proof of your faith." "Proof" means *Dokimion,* as it is used in the Greek. This is a word used in the smelting process for refining and testing precious metals to either remove the impurities or prove the quality of the metal.

Does this sound like us, prophet? Sure it does. So the word Dokimion was a word used to test or see the results of. This is the proof of the process.

Focus with me on Elisha's life. He does his daily work. His moment of initial tests comes when God's call manifested in his life and he is ready to go.

Let's look at the back story of Elisha's history for a moment. Elisha's father was a wealthy farmer. His family lived well and did not bow down to the false god Baal. The family served God, not Baal.

Theirs was a home where God was honored. Theirs was what we would call allegiance to the faith and structure. Remember, this was during the days of ancient Israel.

The quietude of country life and the discipline of hard and useful work were the applications of the prophetic arc upon Elisha's life. His early life was training in habits of simplicity. He was obedient to his parents and God.

Have we lost that ability today? This is the type of training Elisha did to prepare himself. Have we lost the zeal for this training for God as a prophet called to the nations?

This was not luck; this was not by chance. Stop allowing people to make you feel that God had no one else, so He chose you. Learn what to receive and what you are not to allow to be part of your intake. Look again at Elisha's example. This is a great learning experience for us all as prophets.

His prophetic call came while he was working. Notice he was working with his father's servants. Elisha was plowing in the field. He had taken up the work that lay nearest and needed to be done.

As prophetic and apostolic leaders, how often do we want prophets to see this? Work does not belittle us. Work is what builds us. I could simply shout here!

Elisha had the skills and capabilities of a leader to guide and raise up prophets. He also had the meekness of one who is ready to serve, which is what we all need as prophets.

Working where he was at gave his life a backstory of being steadfast with integrity. He was a man who had the love and fear of God. He was humble as he gained strength of purpose and character.

This was his backstory and is why he became the prophet he became. This is the lesson we learn about the initial tests. Read this again. We all must learn this.

The lessons of his life as God employed that prophetic arc process is that he constantly increased in grace and knowledge, while co-operating with his father in the home with life duties.

He was learning to co-operate with God. This is what God does to and in our lives. He puts us in places and situations. Yes, prophet, this is what God does.

Elisha who was faithful in the little things was preparing for weightier trusts, moment by moment and day by day, through practical experience.

Let me welcome you to the prophetic, where God grooms us for greater works. Tell God thank you right now for the greater works that you will do. Thank Him for allowing you to pass your initial test of your mantle.

Right now, take inventory. Be honest with yourself. Are you ready to serve in a greater role? Ready to serve at a higher level? Do you process the capacity to employ greater works in your life? Prophets, this is a lesson for all of us. What does your initial test reveal?

None of us can know God's purpose in how He moves and does in our lives. One thing for sure, every prophet can be certain: faithfulness in the little things is evidence of fitness for greater responsibilities.

Prophet, know that every act of our lives revels our character. The seer should not be ashamed or try to prove themselves in small duties. We become candidates to be honored by God with higher service *(2 Timothy 2:15)*.

You will have small tests of your character and many other areas of your life as a prophet. Believe that it will happen. Do not be the type of prophet who feels no consequence of how they perform the smaller tasks.

I challenge you to find a person or a prophet you can relate to in the Bible. Once you do that, notice their life and the test you see. Some are big, while some are small. Look to see how your biblical prophet proves fit for an honored position.

Our issue today is that we have prophets who may think themselves fully competent to take up the larger duties. We must see that God looks deeper than the surface.

Elisha's prophetic arc positioned him for a back story that produced a readiness to serve God's call upon his life. Let's look at this as a path for prophetic boots, which represents *readiness for the gospel of peace (Ephesians 6:15)."*

Notice that Elisha knew who he was. He is focused on his following throughout. Daily, he was committed to his family. Watch him now as the prophet comes forth.

Elisha is ready to spring up and take action. Notice that he prepared himself where he was; He developed the right habits. Does this speak to you, prophet? Is this you, prophet, responding to God's call with a willing and generous heart? I asked again because this is critical to establish a new commitment to God.

Elisha knows that he is embarking on a new way of life. He will not return to this way of life again. Prophet, are you ready or still trying to decide if it is worth it? How many of us have committed an act that speaks of our commitment to God?

I am not talking about trying to impress anyone, but an act that symbolized your commitment to prophetic ministry and growth. What do you have that you are willing to lay aside for the work of God?

Today, how many of us are willing to lay aside anything for the work of God? This is what is required of the prophet. Have you passed this test yet?

I have a question for you, my prophetic friend. How far do you want to go in God? It will depend on how you're tested and how you respond to the tests. *Luke 9:62* says that no one who puts his hand to the plow and looks back is fit for service in the Kingdom of God. We must move forward prophet.

The example of Elisha and Elijah is a great standard bearer for prophets, as we speak of tests. Like Elisha, your initial test in your calling will be what you are willing to leave behind. *1 Kings 19:19-21* is where Elijah got his commission to raise up Elisha.

God told him to go and receive Elisha, son of Shaphat, as a prophet. Watch this, as we now have 60 years of ministry starting. Elisha is in the field, plowing with twelve yoke of oxen.

Elijah now walked up to him and threw his mantle around him. This was a test for Elisha. He immediately then left his oxen and ran after Elijah. What is going on here? Maybe a better question is, can he have time to kiss his parents goodbye? Elijah tells him to "Go back."

This is Elisha's initial test. God is using Elijah to test Elisha. When God calls a prophet, they will be initially tested and expect the test to be quick. Elisha wants to go with Elijah, but Elijah says, "Go back."

Notice the events here. Elijah replies, "What have I done to you?" So, in light of that, Elisha left him. He now goes back to get his affairs in order. Today, we call it the prophet's red file, which is the personal affairs of the prophet. Notice that Elisha took his yoke of oxen and slaughtered them to prepare a goodbye dinner for himself and the others.

He burned his equipment to cook the meat and gave it to those he was working with. Test after test. What are you willing to leave behind? Read this lesson and reread it until it sinks in.

The key to understanding this is the "mantle" of Elijah. Elijah's mantle indicated he was a prophet. Can you see it now as Elijah comes up and throws his mantle around Elisha?

Elisha didn't have to ask, "What's going on?" because he knew he was prepared. He knew exactly what that meant. Mantles were typically made of animal hair and worn by kings and prophets. Remember that a mantle can also represent a gift.

'Mantle' used here is symbolic. This is how people of status were identified. A prophet's very special status was seen in that person's mantle.

So, Elisha didn't have to ask Elijah what was going on. He knew he had been called. This was a validation of Elijah's status and Elisha's calling. Elisha now interprets Elijah's action as a request to become his servant/disciple, for he asks permission to say goodbye to his parents, and then he will follow.

Elijah continues the enigmatic scene by saying, in essence, "No one is stopping you." Elisha returns, feeds his people, and follows Elijah as his servant.

Elisha's service with Elijah paved the way for his future prophetic role. What transpires between them sounds similar to the occasion when Jesus declared, "Follow me," to His disciples.

One asked to bury his father first. In *Matthew 8:21*, Jesus said, "Let the dead bury the dead." Let the spiritually dead bury the physically dead, but the implication is that he was really offering an excuse to Jesus' call to discipleship. How many of today's prophets are full of excuses?

The story is so familiar. The potential prophetic disciple promises to follow and yearns to be exposed to the surface of the prophetic but may not at all be sold out to the behind-the-scenes farewells and letting go of issues that remind us of Elisha plowing. As we discussed, these contradictions previously.

This may sound tough and it should because it is. This is why the prophetic arc has been employed upon our lives to teach and give us a deposited experience.

As prophets, we spend time counting the cost. There is a real seriousness of Elisha's response. When Elisha received his call as the mantle of Elijah touched his shoulders, he knew it contained a promise of the endowment of the power of God.

This is the product of a relationship with God. He knew faith that could not be tested was faith that could not be trusted.

How seriously did Elisha take this call from Elijah? Just look at this again. We see a great example of someone leaving behind the old life when the call of God comes. I have asked this question several times, is this you? We must be sure.

A key point in times of testing is to be like Elisha. He knew this was a new beginning for him and there is no compromise with his past life.

There was no looking back here! How about you prophet? Have you been looking back prophet? Ask yourself, are you pressing on to the higher calling of our Lord?

The ministries of Elijah and Elisha supplement each other. They are different. God uses different personalities and prophets in different ways at particular times.

Prophets consider that with such a call as Elisha received to succeed the great prophet Elijah, we imagine that he would soon become quite prominent. This is one of the great problems of today's prophets, as we run from ministry to ministry looking for notoriety that may be upon someone else's life. Some prophets run from prophet to prophet, especially if they think that prophet has a name.

We strive to catch it for ourselves. This is our way of doing things and we would rather skip the testing time. The process of understanding the work of the prophetic arc is priceless here.

We fail to see that God does not work that way. The first job the young prophet got was to be a serving man to his master. In *2 Kings 3:11-12,* we read that Elisha "poured water on the hands of Elijah." Can you name three prophets who want to do that for a season of prophetic discipleship?

Today, we have a dictionary of slang terms for that, from fool to flunky. Look how Elisha waited on Elijah, brought the wash basin, and drew the water; thus, a future career of great usefulness began.

This is test after test after test. Your mantle, gift, and servitude must be sure, tried, and tested. Again, I ask you to identify three prophets that you know. Are you one of those three?

Looking at the later results, Elisha must have been faithful and observant, gradually becoming qualified. This was not because he hung around. It was because he worked.

Let us learn the lesson. The call of God is often thrilling. We run over enthusiastically and feel that the time is short, and we must be up and doing.

People respond so tardily, but we, as prophets, would like to shout it on the housetop so that someone will be stirred to meet our needs, recognize us, and send us forth.

Instead, we have to mark time and accept the chastening of our eager spirits until we are really ready. Prophet, right here, the prophetic arc establishes itself. Then God will work, and in His time, you are on your way.

Most prophets never accept or fulfill this test because it is boring and time-consuming. We find ourselves with an unnamed ministry for long stretches in our lives. Does this sound familiar to you prophet?

Tests will be a part of your life as a prophet. Your backstory should be rich with experiences and issues. The day arrived when God decided that Elijah should be removed. Elisha decided that he would not be shaken.

He was going to stay by his master at all costs. Here, we have the test of transition as it plays out in both lives. Again, the prophetic arc is in place.

Elijah tried to shake him off, but the only response he got was, "As the Lord lives, I will not leave thee." He was advised to stay behind three times, but each time, he made the same reply.

As prophets, we set our faces to seek God and then are turned aside by some distraction. Then, we soon discover that we have let down God and going nowhere. We are failing the test.

The prophetic arc of Elisha's life has turned and there is a great lesson. Elisha's determination is to diligently seek. Christ taught the same thing, for in *Luke Chapters 11 and 18*, we are urged to ask, seek, and knock, as the widow who wanted action by the unjust judge.

Change comes through diligence. Who among us prays without quitting or pursuing despite the results? Prophet, do you understand what is needed here for us to succeed?

Elisha wanted the anointing he witnessed of Elijah. Elisha's last journey with Elijah contains some good lessons about what transpires in the heart when tarrying for the baptism with the Spirit.

Here are four key issues that have become standards for prophets to understand in prophetic development. First, let's look at Gilgal, which means rolling away. We get rid of the worldly way of leaning on the arm of flesh and begin a new separated walk in which Christ will prove Himself as "all and in all." This is the place of faith.

The second point is Bethel, the house of God. This teaches abiding. The Spirit-filled life can be lived in no other way, and the sooner we learn it, the better. This is the area of decision. Elisha decided and Elijah would never shake him until God took him.

The third point is Jericho. Here, we are introduced to the "obedience of faith." If God is to work, we must believe. There is no other way.

We pray and pray and do all we can to get the baptism, but faith and praise will make more headway than anything else. This is the warfare area as Elisha is being processed. Jericho is the place where we inherit the warfare of our leaders.

Jordan is the fourth and final point. The plan of God is death to self, or, "Not by might, nor by power, but by the Spirit, said the Lord of hosts." Jordan is crossed; Elisha is still following Elijah. This is when the prophet learns to see!

The moment of truth arrives in Elisha's life. Elijah asked him, "Ask what I shall do for thee, before I be taken from thee." This is the place where he has earned the mantle upon his life. Notice prophet, he is ready yet again.

The young man seizes his opportunity and claims what goes with his call: "I pray thee, as he asked God for a double portion of Elijah's anointed spirit be upon me." Elisha knows he is the eldest son of Elijah.

What he wanted was the portion of the eldest son. His father, Elijah, is to leave him a legacy to become the head of the sons of the prophets.

The custom of the day was to give the eldest son a double portion. This was the understood law for the inheritance, for he became the head of the house when the father died. Elijah, as father, was to be taken, and Elisha must have what goes with his new position.

This tool of the prophetic arc is what God uses in both of their lives. One is up and one is coming up to replace him. Both are put through experiences that necessitate change in their lives. We see them going through things that will be relevant in their lives later.

Elisha had hid in the shadow of the great Elijah. He is trained to impact the world with his ministry in a larger way than Elijah *(2 Kings 2-9 and 13)*. The process is so beautiful if we would only follow it.

What does the prophetic arc teach us about Elisha?

1. Prophet, understand that it will always cost something to follow the call of God. To walk this path is not easy, and you must stop running from tests.
2. Elisha was positioned to understand that God was his source. Prophets, love to connect with power and status, like a mantle or ordination. The reality he learned was that it is the work of God through you.
3. Prophet, the "seen" is easier to identify than the invisible Spirit of God. Elisha's struck the Jordan River and nothing happened. Elijah knew the real power came from God.

The second time Elisha struck the river, the waters parted. A prophet's empowerment does not come from positions or ordination credentials, but from God through His special servants.

We must realize that if you walk with God, you will have issues because He will put you in a position to be crushed. God puts us in these positions not because He is angry, but because He is giving us the integrity of life to live out.

Without the integrity of life, the prophet will never understand the prophetic arc and never produce a track record of dealing with tribulations, which produces a back story. Let's talk now about the integrity of life for a prophet in relationship to the prophetic arc.

CHAPTER 7

THE INTEGRITY OF LIFE FOR A PROPHET

Sometimes, it is hard to understand all the elements that go into placing the prophetic arc in relation to the integrity of life. Rest assured, they are deeply intertwined concepts.

So often, the prophet is seen as a moral measuring stick on earth for the things of God. Throughout history, prophets have called societies back to the principles of justice, compassion, and righteousness.

We see our personal process of the prophetic arc, which takes us through various stages of life. The prophet will see their words and actions aimed to restore integrity to human issues when corruption, oppression, and injustice seek to undermine them.

This is important because it is the prophetic voice with a profound sense of divine correction. This is why understanding the focus of the prophetic arc is critical. This is why the back story comes into focus. The prophet now can focus on how and why things happened in their life.

The prophetic arc exposes that prophet to their sense of moral conviction. This is often done through trial and error in a prophet's life. The learning curve of the prophet arc is in play as the prophet experiences multiple ups and downs in their life.

Look at Moses, Abraham, Samuel, and so many others. Looking into their lives, we see the qualities they developed. They developed an immense courage to speak the truth within themselves. This is the process of building the inner man and being true to oneself and God.

So often, the risk of great personal tragedy plays out in a prophet's life as the skills of moral order awaken to uphold sacred values and defend the vulnerable. Throughout scripture, the prophet is the champion of equality and human dignity.

The prophet is sent by God to remind us that integrity is not mere honesty, but a wholeness of character. This is why the development of a prophet deals with the personal moral fiber of these principles despite the pressure to compromise.

A life of integrity for a prophet means that the prophet's actions consistently reflect our deepest values and convictions. This result from the prophets' back story and reflection on what and where God has taken the prophet.

Let us not forget that prophets are imperfect humans who "prophesy in part." The word of the prophet must be discerned. This process is through accountability to the work given by God to a much broader community. Prophet, you are watched whether they talk to you or not. This is a fact.

Within the realm of the integrity of life, we see the prophetic arc and the back story establish the pureness of love within a prophet. The prophetic without love and humility will breed division.

My prophetic friends, we clearly have enough of that today. The fact is cut and dry. Prophetic integrity requires the prophet to be open to different perspectives while remaining rooted in the prophetic arc, which bends the prophet toward justice.

Ultimately, the prophetic arc speaks to us individually and collectively to examine our lives and societies, but the prophet is the first partaker. This can be a moral hurricane as we wrestle with our personal emotions and convictions.

The prophetic arc and a prophet's backstory will adjust the prophet's life to the integrity of life. We all know biblical prophets who courageously spoke truth to power and called people back to righteous living. This is not an easy test or action by any means.

Moses spoke with integrity by confronting Pharaoh's oppression. He led the Israelites out of slavery in Egypt. This caused great personal risk and hardship. The integrity of life is revealed in God's laws and covenant with unwavering commitment by Moses.

Nathan the Seer and Prophet boldly confronted King David about his adultery. Speaking of personal risk, his status as a prophet weighed heavy as he spoke to David about Bathsheba and the murder of her husband, Uriah.

There was not one time when Nathan shied away from holding David accountable. Do you still want to walk in this walk? The personal risk can be great, as you work for God.

We see the prophet Jeremiah as he suffered persecution and imprisonment. He claimed God's judgment on Judah's rampant idolatry and social injustices. Jeremiah's hardship was exemplified as a critical part of his prophetic calling, which he ministered for at least 40 years.

John the Baptist epitomized prophetic integrity of life as he publicly rebuked King Herod for marrying his brother's wife, an act which ultimately led to his beheading. He shows us real prophetic integrity as he did not compromise his moral convictions despite threats.

Then there was the prophet Amos, a simple shepherd. He was an outsider, but he was bold. We see that Amos condemned the wealthy elite of Israel for their oppression of the poor and lack of ethical conduct.

We see prophet after prophet, called by God, as they became the standard bearers of their time. God's prophets define the integrity of life in that specific season. We even see John the Revelator, who remained faithful to his prophetic witness in a corrupt world.

The prophet of God must exemplify God's profound integrity. We must align our words and actions with God's eternal truths. To my prophetic peers, as you read this, understand that it may mean opposition and suffering. Do you have the prophetic courage and moral conviction today? Yes, I am asking you a fair question.

Prophet, understand that one of the hardest things you will ever do is become successful. Success is a process of transition. *Joshua Chapter 1* enlightens us about the process of 'Good Success' in a prophet's life.

We see God spoke to Joshua about this very fact three times. Joshua was the recipient and the replacement for Moses. Joshua 1:8 alerts us that Joshua is on the verge of a major transition, and he needs God's investment to realize his promised 'Good Success.'

We look at God speaking to Joshua about how to have good success. Those of you who are prophets, seers, watchmen, apostles, and even 5-fold ministry gifts, listen and heed this assignment. There is integrity in this type of life that God wants to instill in His prophets.

Success is one of the hardest things you will ever deal with or even realize as a prophet. Your peers and people generally will not hate or be jealous of you when you fail to pursue success.

The flip side says differently. Let us understand this is the integrity of life as a prophet. Success is doing something that others may not ever do.

There will be haters when you are successful. Often, these haters will not talk to you, but they will talk about you. In other words, success brings you gossipers and enemies you never knew.

Real prophetic success will make you a loner even among other people and, yes, even other prophets. Ask Jeremiah, Moses, Joseph, and David.

Ladies, ask Deborah, Mariam, Hilda, or Anna. Here is a question for you to consider. Do you really think Moses did not have enemies or haters within the 3 million people he led?

Please do not fool yourself. Ask yourself, can you handle this? The prophetic arc of your life has turned you in a certain direction, and now God has shown you success because you were willing to walk in integrity. Stop complaining about this and walk in your higher calling.

Most prophets spend a great deal of their lives learning how to walk in integrity in the midst of haters and gossipers as God starts to raise them up. The ability to process the transition of learning how to be strong and be of good courage is priceless.

Prophet, the investment of God is communicated from God in your life. There is a quality of life that every prophet aspires to. Look at the investment He makes within Joshua's life.

God speaks to Joshua and warns him that fear will negate his success. This is the integrity of life that he must understand and pass. How many prophets have had their success negated because they feared being different?

Every prophet of God needs to know that fear will destroy their success, as cancer eats away at a person's health. Here, we see that the prophetic arc is a tool that reveals the preparation of the prophet.

This is an inside issue that the prophet faces their fear and they now are faced with a hard reality. Prophets, fear is a spiritual cancer; it will totally destroy your faith.

God wants the prophets to change their attitudes so He can elevate them during the transition. God spoke to Joshua about this as He was about to bless Joshua, but Joshua had to change. Joshua had to be courageous to experience success. This is the will of God in a prophet's life.

There is no integrity of life without transition. We all experience this reality as God divinely trains us in between places. You are away from where you came from but not where you are going.

You are in between; you are in transition. Understand that transition is not comfortable or easy, but through God, it is attainable. Here, you are doing what is not familiar to you. How many are there right now? Things you used to do, you finally broke away, but now you're in a place where nothing is familiar.

You are clearly experiencing the integrity of life, which you have not known. God is showing you much and it can and will be uncomfortable. Do you remember how your grandparents and others, as they used to say, "higher heights and deeper depths?"

This is a reality, and some prophets handle change better than others. This is the downfall of prophets who want to copy their peers and contrast and compare themselves to them.

Learning the integrity of life and managing our mentality can often render us stuck in the middle of nowhere. We stay there, and we call it God. The God we serve is a God that changes us. He introduces us to change to make us better, and we resist it.

So many of us miss the fact that God is working in our lives. We see life as a fairy tale, but we need to see life as an experience of preparation. This is the work of God upon His prophets.

Are you like Joshua? He is changing; he is not debating God on issues; he is in a transition where he has never been. He understands he can't stay on the level he has been at.

Look at *John Chapter 2*. Can you imagine being at the wedding of Canaan? The people are out of wine and have a need. Their need may sound insignificant: a bunch of people who want to get drunk, but Jesus is there.

Understand that Jesus was sensitive to the needs of the people at the wedding. That same sensitivity applies to us as prophets. Just like Joshua, who was around Moses, and now Moses is gone, and you have to transition into a season of understanding the sensitivity of God in a way you never have. Are you there?

The prophetic arc of God has exposed a weakness in your life and God has you there to work on it. I ask again, are you there, and does your situation expose you in a way that only God can strengthen you?

Could the spirit of intimidation have been at work in Joshua's life? We see it so often today. Go back and look at *John Chapter 2:3-5*. They needed wine and Mary, Jesus's mother, spoke to Jesus about the need at the wedding in Canaan. Jesus tells her that his time had not yet come. Think about how important this is.

Mary walks away and tells the servants to do whatever Jesus says. Can you imagine being there and seeing Jesus there? His mom has a request; she speaks it and simply walks away, assuring that He will do it despite His reluctance.

How many of us are walking in that type of faith? This type of faith only comes through the process of going through something. Prophet, you must understand that Mary knew Jesus was the answer to their problem. She knew he would be sensitive to the situation.

Despite what it looked like, she knew Jesus would come through. Prophet, there are people who need to know that you are able to point them to God in a way that reveals the answer to their problems.

Prophet, you are empowered in the image of God to be an answer to someone's problem. The anointing is upon you and you must respond. Prophetic sensitivity is a vital element born of the integrity of life.

Prophetic ministry starts with a human inconvenience where someone is gifted but does not know the basics of their gift. This person is now experiencing some things. The reality is that things they feel one way about, they really see them another way.

This is critical for the prophet to understand as their perspectives change as they grow. The prophetic arc changes them and creates a back story for them to pull from. The prophet will now experience a new reality of life. Why is this important?

When God's people come to you with the same human need that puts a demand on your anointing, their experiences of life make it now come back to you. People now take the liberty to pull and put a demand on your gift. Do not ever forget this prophet.

We, as prophets, function like this. Jesus demonstrated this in the lives of wedding attendees, just as He does in everyday life. This power spurred "Good Success" in Joshua's life. This was his deposited experience that served him so well. His back story was in full effect.

Success and time make for a wonderful relationship in a prophet's life. Time is critical to success, as success is critical to time. There has never been a prophet in scripture who did not respect time; yes, even the prophet Balaam respected time.

Successful people in the secular world will not allow you to waste their time. God's now day successful prophets will not allow their time to be wasted.

The question you need to ask is why? The answer is that the power of time is relevant in a prophet's life. Jesus was gone for 18 years, and now he returns. Everyone, including his mom, are looking to him to provide answers to the dilemma.

Even though Jesus tells his mom it was not His time, He is still sensitive to her wishes, just as God is sensitive to your needs, prophets.

Your ability to develop discipline and mentality takes time. Before you do that, you can run out in the world, but your emotions will destroy your ministry and opportunities.

You can be extremely gifted, still waste time, and not understand why you never developed. Prophet, this is your integrity of life. Ask God for your personal revelation on this very topic.

Prophets and people who do not respect time usually waste time and see nothing wrong with it. Respecting the power of time is the beauty of the integrity of life for a prophet. This part of the prophetic arc is critical in a prophet's life.

We all know an aspiring prophet who never learned the language or principles of prophetic ministry. They ran out and depended on emotionalism and not the timely process of being mentorship under the prophetic arc.

Go back and look at Joshua's life; you will see he put his time in. Successful prophets will now allow time to be wasted, nor will they allow others who waste time in their space. This is an important fact that you must respect.

God respects time, and the prophet who does not will always be frustrated in building a relationship God. You will ask God, and it seems like He does not answer or even acknowledge. Then you go forth anyway because it is what you want to do. Seeking God is a process.

God created time, so you must understand that He respects time. Do you disrespect time? Take an honest inventory of yourself, the prophet. Are we meeting the standard of God's leaders as He leads them to set time?

Are we honorable? Disrespecting and wasting time is not honorable, especially when you see nothing wrong with it. Joshua honored time, and because he did, God spoke into his life and spoke good success. Good success was God's investment into Joshua's life. Prophet, do you want God to invest in your life? If you do, then honor time; do not waste it.

Joshua had seen and witnessed the mantle of Moses in his life, and he did not run away, nor did he argue with God. God repeatedly told him to be strong and of good courage three times to ensure him that He was with him. Transition was upon him.

Every prophet stuck in the same rut must learn to respect time. Time walks with the integrity of life. Time is a tool to build faith and a foundation of wisdom. Prophet, respect time and change the season in your life. Prophet, your good success is monitored by time.

Become a prophet who respects time, and your back story will be a symbol to those who God assigns to your life. They to understand that the prophetic arc upon their lives is there for a reason, and as they experience the integrity of life, they will grow into successful prophets.

God has no respect of people, so stop wasting time and watch yourself grow. Prophet, what is the vision or dream that God has given you? When God gives you a dream or a vision, put a date or dates of competition or progress on it.

For those prophets who want to benefit as the prophetic arc brings them face to face with the integrity of life. Review these 5 Key points. We can look for and expect as time prepares us, as we experience the integrity of life. The integrity of life brings you face to face with everything that we, as prophets, have tried to skip or belittle in our development. Let's look at these important points of reference.

1. We see a prophet who will dedicate themselves and follow God as Joshua did. Take inventory here.
2. We will see a prophet who learns how to keep this promise *(Joshua 6:22–25)*. The integrity of a prophet is critical.
3. We see a prophet who serves God as a soldier of honor *(Joshua 1:5 and Joshua 8:28-29)*. God proved His word in Joshua's life.
4. Joshua now is a prophet whom God uses *(Joshua Chapter 3, 6, 10)*.
5. Joshua is now a prophet who faithfully enacts the Lord's will.

Joshua was a solution to a nation that needed him and sought his gifting. Joshua knew who he was. Prophet, some people will always see you as a problem, no matter how hard you work to become you. They are not your assignment. Greet them and keep going.

Prophet, rest assured that God is taking you through the process because people are looking for you. As you serve, they see you as the answer to their problems.

What part of the prophetic arc will marry your ministry to the purposes of God? Do you have the wisdom to know what is and what is not? Let's take some time and explore the effect of the prophetic arc on prophetic wisdom.

CHAPTER 8

PROPHETIC WISDOM

Wisdom is part of the 7-fold anointing of *Isaiah 11:2*. Wisdom is the principle anointing. It is the principle of prophetic anointing in developing a prophet. For a prophet, the topic of prophetic wisdom has to begin with ignorance.

The ignorance of that prophet will make that prophet seek God for insight. Let me explain. Let's start again by understanding the operation of our individual prophetic arc. Prophet, you are now in a place, where you need to learn and be a sponge for wisdom. This is what the prophetic arc will do if you embrace life with an attitude of gratitude.

The prophet must be willing to learn. A prophet who does not know is a prophet who can absorb the concept of prophetic wisdom. That prophet must be hungry and humble.

A prophet who feels they already know is doomed to repeat the process or they will skip the process and accept failure. Prophetic wisdom is designed by God for prophets who are in transition. Transition is a tool God uses to teach prophets His divine order.

These prophets are identified in the process of being between where they were and where they are going. Prophetic wisdom is for a prophet who seeks to grow in God despite their status.

This prophet is receptive and will learn and employ the concepts of prophetic wisdom. The steps to acquiring prophetic wisdom require a solid strategy employed by the participating prophets. This simply means that the prophet is focused despite what they are going through.

Prophetic wisdom births prophetic influence. An example of this is when God tells Joshua He will magnify him in the eyes of the people. That is influence. You can be a well-known prophet and still not have influence, so understand how important this is. Popularity is not the seed of prophetic wisdom; it is the perceptions of man.

Prophetic wisdom births the influence that the prophet has on those who follow or may know that prophet. God gives His prophets prophetic wisdom as revelation flows out of them to influence everything around them.

Prophet, understand that a wise tongue brings life in dead situations. Prophetic wisdom helps discern the timing, manner, and appropriateness of delivering a prophetic message.

Prophetic wisdom provides the anointing to escort that prophetic message as it comes to pass. Picture prophetic wisdom as the confidence that a prophet speaks with.

Prophetic wisdom establishes the foundation of the prophet's timing and the manner and appropriateness of the prophetic utterance. A prophet's message outputs divine insight and practical guidance on the revelations from God. This is why prophetic wisdom is important.

Look at Jeremiah and understand this. Yes, understand this is what the prophetic arc brings to your life, prophet.

Look at Jeremiah's message to the leaders of Judah in Jeremiah 18. God told Jeremiah to go to the potter's house, where we see Jeremiah display prophetic wisdom.

He brings a message from God. He is humble and attentive as he allows the spirit of God to give him insight as he speaks to the leaders of Judah. His message is a warning of impending judgement wrapped in a prophetic rebuke.

The prophet must understand that prophetic wisdom tempers the delivery of prophecies with love, humility, and discretion to bring healing rather than harm. Let me stress again that this is where your prophetic arc will take you and you must be able to adjust to it.

How do we develop prophetic wisdom? This model must be employable to God's prophets of all levels. Let's talk now about it in the actual sense of how we actually do it. Prophetic wisdom, in the now generation, is clearly needed.

Let's look at doing the following to create prophetic wisdom.

1. **Cultivate a safe environment for the prophet to take risks**. This is a learning environment. Prophets must be allowed to make mistakes and not be judged. Emerging prophets need encouragement.

Many times, some prophets may hesitate to speak because of past situations or they could be intimidated. Help them by creating the correct environment for them to learn in.

2. **Provide training on various prophetic mantle types.** This happens when prophets study how they speak and carry themselves. Monitor their temperament.

This prophet must be allowed to find themselves, which means they should find the prophet in scripture who they relate to the most. This will require study and the prophets in training must be allowed to validate why they feel they relate to them. Insight from prophetic leadership is needed and vital for encouragement and helping guide them.

This will motivate them to study as they learn more about their biblical model prophet. This is important as God will show the prophetic arc of that prophet as we see the ups and downs of that prophet.
 This is a critical step because if that prophet is going to develop, they need a reference point in scripture to help them with that prophet's actions in critical times.

3. **Conduct training in small groups of 3-5 and no more than that if possible.** This will allow more opportunities for prophets to activate their prophetic gifts and get the work they need.

Within a small group, they can receive feedback and discuss how to apply the prophetic word with wisdom and clarity, all under the watchful eye of a seasoned prophetic mentor.

4. **Practice the Three A's**
• **Asset**
Be honest with yourself. Speak with mature, trusted prophetic leaders who know you, your situation, and where you are in your development.
• **Action**

Take action and work on what you need. You can't afford to sit back or allow yourself to become entangled in the world's issues and you neglect your opportunities for growth.

- **Accountable**

Take prophetic words and submit them to trusted prophetic leaders for counsel and interpretation on how to handle the responsibility of being a prophet. This provides the strategy and steps to effectively walk out a prophetic word or direction from God.

5. **The prophet must operate in humility.** This is the key to understanding that the wisdom the prophet seeks comes from God. The prophet must exhibit a humble and hungry-for-God posture.

The posture reflects a healthy heart attitude for the prophet to grow and operate in to apply the needed discernment to steward the prophetic gift. Prophets should always remember that our physical posture can signal if we are aligned with God's Spirit.

Within the prophetic, the spiritual and physical postures both work together to elevate that prophet or keep that prophet in a place of being unteachable.

6. **Learn from your mistakes.** You will make mistakes and you need to understand that you should respond to them with grace. When handled properly, mistakes are learning opportunities in the prophetic.

Mistakes will guide how, when, and why a revelation is shared to maximize its impact and avoid causing harm. Everybody benefits. Mistakes are valuable in the prophet's training and learning.

7. **Cultivate intimacy with God.** The importance of prayer and worship is priceless. This will develop your relationship with God. From the relationship, prophetic wisdom grows and enables us to get a deeper understanding and meaning of the importance of prophetic revelation. In other words, our eyes are illuminated by God to grasp the full significance.

These seven points are why we must seek God's wisdom and partner with the Holy Spirit to steward and respond to prophetic words properly. Prophecies require wisdom to wage spiritual warfare and overcome obstacles.

The prophet must operate in prophetic wisdom for the supernatural insight from God to handle prophetic revelations rightly. It is vital for those with prophetic gifts to seek this wisdom from the Holy Spirit.

Prophet, as we continue to move into the prophetic arc, let's look at the now generation prophet. Every prophet should keep a journal to make notes on themselves. This journal helps them reflect on their growth and self-monitor themselves.

With that being said, you really need a mentor. Mentorship is about you trusting and listening to someone. Today's prophets make a vital error with mentorship as they hear the mentor, but do not listen to them. Understand that you can't eat from everyone's prophetic table.

So many of today's prophets will rebuke correction for the opportunity they feel they must pursue to move forth. This is the main reason many prophets need to find a true mentor.

The prophet must check his or her attitude, because they will not be in agreement with the mentor all the time. Prophet, you also need to understand you will not be in agreement with God all the time either.

The 7 roles as prophetic mentors we will assume will be:

1. Teacher:

As teachers, you can expect us to teach and demonstrate the technical skills unique to the prophetic. Prophets, please understand that the ultimate goal of prophetic education is the formation of your character.

2. Sponsor:

As sponsors, we are tasked to introduce prophets into the prophetic community. The sponsor has a responsibility to be on guard to ensure the emerging prophet is trained and equipped as prophetic interaction commences with other prophets and seers.

3. Advisor:

Our job as mentors is to serve as advisors and counselors. We provide the missing experience, of being there, and done that. Understand that the relationship will and can change depending on the prophet, but the fact that remains of who the mentor becomes in that prophet's life is priceless.

4. Agent:

As prophetic agents, we will stand in the gap for you. We are tasked to remove obstacles, but only after the emerging prophet has made a convincing attempt to show themselves serious.

5. Role model:

The mentor lives so emerging prophets can identify with people with similar attributes and behavior that are fit to be emulated. Prophets and seers simply do not learn values from having them preached at them. This is learned by experiencing and seeing values enacted in the routine of daily lives of other prophets. Values are best transmitted through deeds, not words.

6. The Prophetic Coach

A prophetic coach can motivate a hungry prophet to achieve. They know when to offer encouragement and when to push. The prophetic coach knows when to push for action while tolerating inaction. The prophetic mentor raises the bar and sets high standards. This is the process of going to the next level.

7. The Prophetic Confidante

A prophetic mentor must be a confidante: someone the emerging prophet can talk to, knowing the discussions are kept strictly confidential. This relationship is based on trust.

The mentor wins and sustains the prophet's trust through constancy (staying the course), reliability (being there when it counts), integrity (honoring commitments and promises), and congruity (walking the talk).

Welcome to your prophetic learning curve. Prophetic wisdom gives the prophet the opportunity to learn how to persevere, overcome obstacles, and walk out prophetic revelations in the midst of spiritual warfare.

While this develops the foundation and greatness to establish prophetic wisdom in your life, develop it in your life as a prophet. The prophetic arc delivers again within the prophet's life.

The advent of social media and technology has led many of today's prophets to move away from birthing prophetic wisdom within them and get caught up in the "I can do it too or I hear from God also syndrome" that so many prophets waste much of their lives in.

When this happens, our character suffers and we never understand *1 Corinthians 14:32* tells us that the spirits of the prophets are always subject to the prophets.

This is why we must deal with the process of the prophetic arc of our lives. We find ourselves tossed and turned. Yet, we may not be growing. We live in a generation that looks at us and has lost faith in us.

There is a generation of Christians who are skeptical of us, who need us but can't depend on us as prophets. This is not to sound negative, but to enlighten the prophetic community, we have much work to do.

That is a reality and the only way we can recover is to follow and allow God to prepare us. God's tool of the prophetic arc is needed now more than ever and it is our responsibility as the now day prophetic nation to deal with this present day generation we find ourselves in.

CHAPTER 9

A GENERATION THAT HAS LOST FAITH IN THE PROPHET

We are living in a strange time. We need the prophetic gift now more than ever. We may be aware of how the prophet of today is viewed. We must and we will get our acts together.

Let's start again with the prophetic arc. The prophetic arc is simply crucial and critical in a generation that has seemly lost faith in prophets.

The prophetic arc is a powerful reminder of divine guidance and moral accountability. I pray that you have seen this revelation as you read this book.

Prophet, your role extends beyond simply delivering messages. Has anyone told you that you embody a living connection between the divine and humanity? Do not ever forget this.

Your personal prophetic arc represents a journey of revelation, personal growth, and societal transformation, and everything has been recorded in your backstory.

God has used your prophetic arc to demonstrate how spiritual insight can lead to tangible change, inspiring others to reconnect with their faith and values. Welcome to the now-generation prophetic community.

Yes, my friend, make no mistake, we live in an era of cynicism. Your consistent voice and exemplary life will offer a beacon of hope and authenticity. The mere fact that we have prophetic challenges is due to our prophetic arc. It challenges the status quo and that is what our calling does.

The prophetic arc challenges the status quo and calls for societal renewal in the one and true living God. The prophet is an inside figure. We are in the world, but we are not of the world.

Prophet, think about this. You have the unique ability to critique existing systems while remaining connected to the traditions of the world.

The ability to address complex moral and societal issues is priceless. We must model a life deeply rooted in spiritual practice and show that true transformation begins with inner work on ourselves.

Prophet, understand that your prophetic arc bridges timeless wisdom and contemporary needs, offering a path for spiritual revival and societal progress in a skeptical age of people.

Consider this, as a prophet, do you ever wonder if something is wrong with the people or is it you? Maybe someone has worked roots or practiced witchcraft on you?

You may have even sought ungodly help for your situation prophet. This is a shame but some prophets do seek ungodly help.

We need to consider what has happened to you. What was so promising for you and about you?

Now prophet, here you are so sure you're on your way to divine success, and people have lost faith in you and your personal life has become a nightmare.

You look at yourself and now your confidence is shaken. You're a body of nerves. Your trust in people is extremely low as you have been hurt and wounded on the outside. This does not seem to matter that you're God's prophet and you're lost in your situation.

Guess what? On top of that, your generation has lost confidence in you. You have lost confidence in yourself and mostly, you have lost confidence in God to restore you in this unknown situation.

This situation seems unfair. The demonic field generals of frustration and depression are leading the charge against you as you minister to the nations. This is not all glamorous, as many would think about prophets called to the nations.

Do not forget there is another highly critical issue. This is the issue that you're still on the front line for God. People are coming to you for prayer, as you're ministering to them, laying hands and the nightmare of your life makes you feel that you're living two separate lives.

You feel like they have lost confidence in you and wonder why God is taking you through this. This may not be your exact story. Your story may be worse in many ways. You're in a public crisis. You can't understand why God is allowing you to go through this.

Welcome to the life of a prophet when a generation you're as-signed to does not believe you. Hell is breaking loose in your life. Let me say again that the prophetic arc upon your life is there for a reason and not entertainment.

Jeremiah, Moses, Joseph, Daniel, Huldah, and other prophets dealt with this. You wonder where God is and you're facing all this. Yet, God is still sending you forth to His people. You're doing everything you can do.

You have danced, spoken in tongues, worshiped, and tithed. Now your life is still in a crisis on public display. You ask God why? It does not seem like He answers. *Mark 9:9-30* opens us up to such a dilemma.

You will need to read this for yourself. Imagine Peter, James, and John, the chosen Apostles, on the Mountain of Transfiguration with Jesus.

They have seen the Glory in ways no others have ever seen it. They are full of the experience, yet they run into a demon when they return. Imagine that they have been to a special place and now they must deal with a situation that's been put before them.

Have you ever wondered why you go to a meeting and God moves mightily and then in the same breath, you run into some trouble that makes no sense to you, considering where you have just been in God? Elijah could tell us this story well from first-hand knowledge.

Prophets, please think about this. In the meeting, there were souls saved, redeemed, and deliverance. Then an old enemy shows back up in your life. You even remember this enemy called doubt or depres-sion. Maybe it is his 1st cousin called pride or inflated self-worth.

Whatever the case, your old foe you need to defeat has arrived. While you say not now, this is not the time, the fact of the matter, he has arrived.

Old enemies you have battled, now they are here, yet again. You start to wonder when the people said it was not God. Perhaps, you had done something wrong. You were being punished. This is the mental battle the world brings to you prophet.

Many have doubted you and the power of God. You saw and experienced God move and now they have robbed you, yet again of the opportunity of growth in Christ.

Where is your backstory prophet? Did you forget it? Think about where God has brought you from prophet. Welcome to the prophetic, where we grow on the inside before we grow on the outside.

Look at *Mark 9* and consider the experience of a lifetime. The anointing is still on you and if you're Peter, James, and John, you can't rebuke the dumb spirit out of the boy. They just came down from the mountain, full of the Glory of God.

They now face an issue that makes them look ineffective. Can you imagine what's going through their minds?

In *Mark 9: 28-29,* the disciples asked Jesus why they were ineffective. Can you imagine how many people witnessed this and ran their mouth. This is why your focus has to be on God.

There are two valuable lessons learned. **Number one:** they learned that they still had more work to do to continue developing. **Number**

two: they learned that they had not seen everything yet. These two points are priceless and valuable to the prophet's prophetic growth.

Here is where your prophetic arc and backstory come to life. Know that there are two different worlds here: the Glory and the earth reality. Many times, we confuse them. We feel they should work as one and yet, we see a generation so against submitting to God. I wonder how many of you can receive that.

A fellow prophet, along the road of life discovers what you have found upon the narrow road of life. The prophetic arc brings us to this phase.

As a prophet, you will have to go through it, to get to it. This, my friend, is relevant to our development of the prophetic gift. Let's look on the surface. Consider why people come to our revivals, meetings, watch our videos, and want our training. Then they leave us.

They say things about us because on the surface, things may look a certain way. The reality is that those things you think may not be true. This is how church folk and the Body of Christ operate.

Terms they use to describe us are false prophets, money hungry, spiritual peddlers, ineffective, they don't know God, Apostles and prophets were only in the old testament days. Oh the awful things they often say. How thick is your skin?

How ignorant and uninformed we choose to be in the Body of Christ. This is the now generation we live in and why no matter how good you try to be to them, there will always be a group that finds fault with you.

Prophet, be reminded of *Mark 9:18.* The Father speaks, "I came to your people and they did me no good." Today, we say, "I went to the prophet, and all they wanted was my money." Then they say the prophet just stared at me and did not give me a good word, or they did not have a word for me.

How many times have we heard that? Or they did not believe what the prophet said, and they went out telling everybody. They did not mentioned how you gave a big offering, but they put down the prophet regardless.

What happens, prophet, when in that same meeting you experienced the Glory upon your life and the haters are still hating on you? They were still calling you funny names and said you dressed funny. They were still criticizing you and the Glory was upon you. Now they are sending people to you just to see what you will say to them.

The issue is they don't believe and need more fuel for the fire of their unbelief. This makes them feel good about themselves and if you're weak, they will wreck or destroy your mentality.

They secretly covet your gift and yet mock you to ignite the spark of unhealed or unsettled issues in your life. Why would God put you in this situation?

So, prophet what do you do when this happens and all you know is that you done your best? What do we do prophets when this happens, and everyone is looking at the prophetic gifts and they are a huge critic of the mouthpiece of God?

There is much to consider, and we will discuss this from another angle in the next chapter as we discuss our critics. This is your life prophet.

Let's look again at the father who brought his child for healing and is now standing before Jesus. He describes his situation to Jesus. He criticizes John, Peter, and James, just like they criticize us sometimes.

This man is frustrated and irritated. He has been before the front-line men of God of his day, and nothing has happened. Jesus is presented with this and asks him a simple question: How long has the child been like this?

What you must understand is that the people of that day talked also. Imagine the talk about who the disciples were supposed to be. Just like today, people talk no matter how much you encourage them to shut their mouths to things they know little or nothing of. The reality is they are going to talk. They talk now and surely, they talked then.

This is not about them on the mountain. This is about how the people felt and the missing element of little or no faith at all. Stop here and consider their perspective.

Also, notice that the child's condition has affected those close to him. Now, the family as a whole is frustrated. As you can imagine, they wondered why there seems to be no help. Yet the question Jesus answered them is critical. Jesus does not look at the demon. He turns to the father. The father answers since birth.

Do you mean that since this child was born, we see this as a norm? Nothing has been done about it until now because it is only now at a crisis stage for the family. Why did they wait, and now that it is a crisis, you feel he is going to die, now you bring him before Jesus?

So many times, we wait until crisis time, and we want miraculous results and do not have the faith to experience it. In *Mark 9:19,* we see Jesus answered him. Jesus said, *"O faithless generation, how long shall I be with you? How long shall I suffer you? Bring him unto me."* Imagine the demon who now is tearing the clothes of the child in the presence of Jesus.

Jesus is asking the father, "How long have you chosen to live like this? This issue is that Jesus is more interested in the father at this point and we may ask why. Read *Hosea 4:6* and reread it. There is a revelation there that I want you to see for yourself.

The issue is that in order to fix the son with his dumb spirit, we need to consider his father, and what has been allowed to prosper in the lives of his family.

Remember and consider this a generational issue. Have we taught our kids or grandkids what we have allowed just so we could get along? Consider the behavior of some of our children; it is never an issue until it is in the crisis stage.

Today, so often, we see a generation of people who come to the prophet for relief, and the issue is that they don't really believe. They come with an attitude that speaks a loud message. It says if you're who you are supposed to be then this must happen this way.

They have no faith. They depend on relying on your name prophet. They want to dictate the terms and conditions of how they want to be healed and set free.

The issue is when prophets get caught up in this simply because of a lack of faith actually on both sides of the issue. What I am saying is that we must see the base issue in order to get to the root of the issue. This is the prophetic arc shifting our lives in a place that every now generation prophet needs to be aware of.

When people and the things they want don't go the way they want them to go, they blame the prophet. They fan fires of doubt and disbelief. They cause people to adopt attitudes about a gift, so many clearly do not understand.

Some prophets, maybe someone you know, will now withdraw or go into hiding. They feel shame, guilt, and the spirit of intimidation. This hinders the development and it looks like God has forgotten that prophet. Has this already happened to you? If not be mature enough when it does to recognize it. This is what the prophetic arc does for us. It creates a backstory of relevance within our lives.

Why do we live in a generation of people who won't do the basic work of a Christian? Will you come and expect a miracle when your faith is not operating at a miracle level?

Then you get mad at the prophet and feed a slew of insults. Public branding to an uneducated generation is now commonplace. How many churches, faiths, and groups of people have we seen this in? Your city and area are not so different. This is the norm.

So now, when your friends you have gossiped with now need to seek God through the prophetic gift, they cannot because they have listened to you or others gossip. They have absorbed your doubt and unbelief. Are you like the child's father? You call it belief when you need a miracle.

In *Mark 9:24,* we see that the child's father speaks. He said as he cried out, with tears, "Lord, I believe; help thou mine unbelief." Read this again carefully. Do you notice in one sentence he says, "He believes, and also says he has unbelief?" Read it again if you need to.

Welcome to the now generation prophets. On Monday you are sent from God and on Wednesday you are not of God. There should be no doubt that we have issues to solve and they need to be solved quickly. God shifts our lives in order to deal with these types of issues. He uses his prophetic arc on our lives prophets.

Look at us. We are so like the father. We are a generation that wants no responsibility. We want to pay no price for the oil we seek upon our lives. We seem to never understand that the anointing costs a great price that so many of us are unwilling to pay.

Look at *Mark 9* again. The father of this child represents both sides of the equation. There is a side of a generation of little or no faith, and there is a generation of prophets who are wounded and God has you in the battle to show you that He is your healer.

This is why we must pay attention to our prophetic arc. We must be knowledgeable to the prophetic arc process as we walk in the extreme level of faith needed for true prophetic development.

We have to know who we are here to serve and understand who we are. God is our deliverer also as we present Him to the world. We are not just a generation that has lost faith in the prophet. We have lost faith in God.

We have acquired many critics along the way and the truth is they will always be there. Let's speak directly to them now! Our prophetic arc protects us.

CHAPTER 10

TO THE CRITICS OF TODAY'S PROPHETS

Throughout this work, my focus has been on showing that the prophetic arc represents the journey and evolution of a prophet's ministry, encompassing their initial calling, life experiences, and impact on others.

Anyone who attempts to truly understand the prophet must know of the prophetic arc and why God has used it as a tool in a prophet's life.

As prophets, we deal with the call upon our lives. We develop and see ourselves thrust into public ministry. We then move into the arena of impact and influence. Here is where we deal with and discover the critics of today's prophets.

Look in the scriptures and you will see multiple prophets who went through this process. They are real and firmly established in how they see and perceive us. They are our critics.

As prophets continue in ministry, their influence grows. Their messages resonate more widely, leading to tangible changes in individuals and communities. This is the prophetic gift in action. This is what the prophet arc and backstory do.

The prophet's legacy, teachings, and work will stand long after that prophet is called home. While the legacy is often preserved through writings, followers, and yes our critics provide a lasting impact.

The modern day prophets face significant criticism, which can be categorized into several key areas. Let's briefly look at each area and understand it because you will not escape it.

Prophetic Accuracy: Our critics will often question the reliability of our prophetic utterances, especially when they fail to come true. Did you ever notice that they set the time when it was supposed to happen or should have happened? We live in an age where information is readily available and easily scrutinized.

Prophetic Motivation: Our critics will have concerns about our motivation as prophets. They monitor us and argue that we are driven by personal gain, fame, or power rather than a genuine prophetic gift.

Prophetic Accountability: Here is a big one, as they see we lack formal oversight. This in turn raises questions about our accountability. We more often than not do not present a structured framework. This can be challenging in the prophetic but is necessary and needed to remain true to the calling of the prophet.

Theological Consistency versus the Prophetic Gift: Sometimes, our prophetic utterance may be seen as contradictory to established religious teachings. This inconsistency can lead to confusion and division within religious communities. Yes, we see this a lot as our critics speak of us.

Social Impact of the Prophet: Our influence as prophets is a strong area of concern. Critics worry that prophetic utterances can lead to extreme beliefs or behaviors, potentially causing harm to individuals and communities or believers of various faiths. This is real and can't be overlooked.

We can also add personal prophetic leader experiences and untrained prophets to this list and we can keep adding if we so desire. As the now generation prophets, we must be aware of criticism and learn how to deal with it. Education in our circles and groups is essential and needed.

Two things I have found that are effective in dealing with critics are humility and transparency about the prophetic process. This way, you alert your onlookers to God. You are not moved by what you see, but by what you believe.

When people interact with you prophet, they look for spiritual discipline, accountability, and the opportunity to learn from you, as you are the symbol of their relationship with God.

This commitment to growth can enhance your credibility and impact. This is what people do as they pull from the prophetic mantle. Let us explore the fact that many of our ancestors, tended to kill prophets, especially those who did not fit into their so called and unnamed circles of influence.

Real prophets of God have little patience for our categories, parties, factions, and niches. God's martyrs don't fall so nicely into the worldly categories.

Luke 11:48-52 says, "Woe to you because you have built tombs for the prophets. Your fathers who killed them. Now you testify that you approve of what your forefathers did?" God speaks with His wisdom saying, "I am going to send them prophets and apostles. Some of whom they will kill and others they will persecute."

This is the generation being held responsible for the blood of all the prophets that has been shed since the beginning of the world, from the blood of Abel to the blood of Zechariah, who was killed between the altar and the sanctuary. Prophets have been killed and have suffered for God. Remember, we are servants.

For a true prophet of God, this is pretty much the norm for prophets. Jeremiah, who was cast into prison for being "unpatriotic." In *Jeremiah 37-38,* he prophesied that the Babylonians would conquer the Israelites if Israel did not repent.

Prophets just don't fit in. Prophets will break through political distinctions and tend to offend just about everyone. This is the integrity of life for us that we face and must deal with.

Today, so many prophets suffer from being killed by reputation and character mixed with gossip and slander by the people to whom God sent them. Physically and spiritually, the unspoken goal is to demoralize them.

Today, we see this society will abort a child and kill a prophet spiritually and by reputation and relationship. While within the prophetic, we like to make distinctions, the reality is that being dead still means being dead. No prophet is no less dead in their imperfection than a child in their innocence. The reality is that we all have critics.

Hebrews 13:13 shows that Jesus, our savior, was crucified "outside the gate" to symbolize that he fit nowhere in Israel's little systems or categories. Can you see that Jesus was hated by all the political parties of his day? The Sadducees, the Pharisees, and others agreed on nothing, but the fact that Jesus had to go.

Many prophets have constituents and comrades and we need and should be covenant partners. When they see us not together, it is much easier to destroy us as maverick prophets or renegade prophets.

These are supposed to be our Christian brothers and sisters. They do and will bring forth the multiple charges against us. We will be called physics, money grubbers, fakes, and robbers. Those are some of the nice names the prophet has been given. Prophets, you are going to attract criticism from multiple areas.

Allow me to name at least 7 areas you should be concerned about and expect your critics to be active in these areas. Learn this reality of the integrity of life for a prophet.

1. Your prophetic peers and those who want to be your peers.
2. Those who follow you and or you may mentor them.
3. Those who hate the prophetic ministry for whatever reason.
4. Those who don't understand the prophetic ministry because of denominational bias or are called to a different gifting or work.
5. Those who have been hurt by the prophetic ministry.
6. Those in authority and influence feel they have a right to control or manipulate your gift for their benefit.
7. Seducing Spirits sent by satan to destroy what God is doing within your life.

Prophet, sometimes our critics are right and have valid points. They attempt to point out something wrong that will sniffle our growth. You must know who you are.

Many times, prophets will become unglued. We don't know how to handle ourselves and want our displeasure to pass as proof of Godly authority.

The reality is that as you look at our history you see, the prophets were not perfect. Moses was a murderer. David was an adulterer. Isaiah went about preaching naked. Jonah was reluctant and an ultra-nationalist. We have history, to say the least.

Paul had a bad temper and murdered Christians. Jacob was a shyster. Peter was inconsistent and a denier. We seem to want to insist that prophets must be sinless and have no struggles. That is just not true.

To our distractors who bark loudly about our shortcomings and concerted efforts, they should be sure that what is actually swept under the table is not mentioned, put away, and allowed to die out. Let's all say amen.

Every pulpit everywhere has some issues, but it's so sad that today's saints love rumors, and unsubstantiated information to keep themselves relevant with their brothers or sisters in Christ. What your gossiping friend says is not the word on someone's struggles, just because they are cool with you.

We need to be very careful. The measure we measure to others will be measured back to us *(Mat. 7:2)*. Only the merciful will obtain mercy *(Mat. 5:7)*. God does not forgive us if we do not forgive.

A good prophet will love God's people. As prophets, we are likely to afflict others. This is who we are. We simply do not fit perfectly into situations that seem to think we should conform to a way-out side of God's chosen path and destiny.

Do we have problems? Yes, we do. We have false prophets among us. They come to you in sheep's clothing, but inwardly, they are ferocious wolves. The scripture says that by their fruit, you will recognize them. Grapes don't come from bushes, and every good tree bears good fruit, but a bad tree bears bad fruit.

Many of our haters have problems with us as prophets because the fruits of our actions will not necessarily be in a certain church, area, or event. God chose to work in His way and their way not be the main way many see us working.

Rest assured our haters and critics of the prophetic are not the judge and jury of God's plans. They are only voices among the crowd, and not the voice we listen to prophets.

Prophet, it is horrifying and embarrassing to see prophetic gifts intimidated and ineffective because someone exercises a perceived influence that is not tested or trusted. It is only perceived.

These are the same voices in our society who call for unity and togetherness in the Body of Christ and it's okay if they do what they want to do when they want to do it. Prophet, your prophetic arc will launch you into a reality that you will flourish in as long as you trust God.

Today's prophets should be horrified, but the blame must be shared, as many in our prophetic ranks have decided to move forth untrained and undisciplined.

This foolishness is within our ranks and it must stop. Can you see it as food for the critics and does it keep them talking about us and not God?

We are part of the Body of Christ and among the 5-Fold ministry ascension gifts. Ignoring us and trying to assault our character is not God's way. Nowhere is that God's way in His word. To our brothers and sisters who critique and attempt to demoralize God's prophets, my questions are simple.

Are there not enough secular opponents and critics that we must do this to one another? Who is really praying for who and with who? Where is our faith in the Body of Christ?

Prophets, we must work within our ranks and get them in order. In *Deuteronomy 13,17, 18,* we see syncretism. This echoes many of our inner prophetic struggles among ourselves as prophets and destroys our trust in ourselves.

Syncretism is the work of people who claim to be prophets but attempt to control the future by magical means such as human sacrifice, divination, soothsaying, omens, sorcery, spells, mediums, and necromancy.

The emphasis here is on human initiative in trying to control the world. The world rejects the very concept of faith in God, His grace, and His providence for the human-controlled world.

Prophet, look how leaders look at us. See what they feel, and seek to move on common ground if at all possible. Be true to who God has raised you to be.

Know who you are and know those who labor among you. Any prophet who advocates any gods must be a false prophet, no matter how many signs they can perform or how accurate their predictions might be.

This is not hard to understand, as we see jealousy, envy, and lack of self-esteem. We also see spiritual leaders who spend quality ministry time downing prophets without taking quality time to see who they are.

The reality that many prophets have to face is this. We have thousands of people who will claim the title of prophet and constantly contradict one another. These prophets believe themselves to be 100% correct.

Apostle Paul gives us some clues we need to look at. In *Acts 17:10-12,* the brothers immediately sent Paul and Silas. They went into the Jewish synagogue.

Apostle Paul was constantly harassed and followed by men who wanted to shut him down for what he taught. Today, as prophets, we face this same issue in the Body of Christ.

Prophets must know what they are talking about. It's that simple. We will be monitored and scrutinized on social media and within certain groups and select faiths. We simply need to know what we know, and it involves getting the proper training.

Paul didn't seem to mind that his words and teachings were scrutinized, as ours will be also. Many of our critics will say we are not interested in this or that, like growing in the word or being mentored. Take heed; this is why the prophetic arc is in place by God.

To a degree, our critics are correct, but they must realize that many within their ranks are doing the same as our immature, uneducated prophetic gifts and while they deserve the same attention we get, it does not seem to happen. So understand we can't worry about that, nor do we control that. Prophets, do the work you need to do to become the best version of yourself.

To those of you who say we don't need prophets today, I simply say that whatever Bible you're reading and teaching clearly are not in line with the 5 Ascension gifts of *Ephesians 4.*

This is not meant to be a debate. There is nothing, we, as prophets, need or care to debate. We are here to stay, and God does and still has work for us to do *(Jeremiah 29:11).*

Prophets understand that our biggest problem with our critics is that we still have not learned how to react to them. Many prophets deal with harsh critics. They can be a powerful force if you allow them.

Successful prophets have learned how to function with hard work. They handle critics and leave at peace with them. Understanding the most important voice we have is the voice of God protecting us from the potential harm of external critics because it is the voice of our destiny.

Here are three ways to build that Teflon tough skin and learn to shield yourself from negative outside forces that undermine your sense of worth.

1. Understand how to process what you are given, the constructive from the destructive. Prophet, your critics come in many forms. Some are easier to recognize than others.

Constructive criticism is healthy and necessary in many situations. If we don't know our weaknesses, how will we ever grow or change?

However, there is a difference between constructive criticism meant to help and unsolicited negative criticism meant to hurt. The key is learning to decipher and process.

Internet trolls today have become almost superhuman as they spend countless hours posting and spreading substantiated rumors, gossip, and information that is intended to harm and degrade the prophetic office and other 5-fold ministry gifts.

Their hurtful remarks are simply a reflection of their own lack of self-compassion. Whether your criticism comes from a troll or an acquaintance, keeping this factor in mind is essential to certain aspects of your growth.

Whether it's a fair-weather friend or the media trying to convince you that you're not good enough, there will never be a shortage of critics to challenge your sense of worth.

2. Be mindful and understand how to process an insult. When someone says something hurtful to or about a prophet, the prophet may be so caught off guard that we don't realize what's happening until after we've had time to reflect or until a friend or a prophetic mentor points it out to us.

The knee-jerk reaction in a moment of criticism or insult is often to believe them and question ourselves when, in fact, we should be doing exactly the opposite.

The next time you question yourself based on another's words, take a moment to breathe, allowing a space between the automatic reaction to take it in as truth.

You are not under obligation to accept an insult, especially if it is not true. What is not true is critical as you consider the source. Remember to consider the source the next time you feel the sting of a negative remark.

The critic will point out how one stumbles. This critic strives to inform about the one who comes short repeatedly. This critic does not understand that there is no effort without error and shortcomings. We are all human.

Prophet, continue to spend time in devotions and seek God for discernment in achievement. Learn how to fail and process it in a cold world. Understand this prophet, and ask yourself if your critic has earned the right to offer criticism. Is this someone you admire or even respect?

3. Finally, thank them for pushing you to the next level.

Prophets, it will do you a world of good to think of your detractors as helpers or teachers there to keep your ego in check. The next time you come across one, thank them and say, "I hear you, but I'm good. Thank you for your concern."

Those who throw us our greatest challenges can be our greatest teachers. Thank and admire them. Prophets, please understand that as sure as there will always be death and taxes, there will always be naysayers in your life.

Accepting this as a fact of life is your safest option, as is recognizing that regardless of how much energy you exert to elicit support from those around you. Some are simply incapable of offering that support. Trying to please everyone all the time is a surefire setup for disappointment.

We are all on separate journeys. We just need to stay in our own lanes. Trust yourself that you are doing your best and never let another's lack of security steal your own.

Finally, you must see that your prophetic arc is a dynamic journey that involves growth, challenges, and renewal. Modern prophets, despite facing significant criticism, can maintain their gifts and impact by staying true to their calling.

We practice humility and demonstrate the practical benefits of our message. By navigating these challenges, prophets can offer their generation valuable spiritual insights and moral guidance, fostering a deeper connection to the divine and promoting societal transformation.

I would be remiss if I did not acknowledge that while some will read this, some will still feel a need to remain in a state of darkness. The prophetic arc in your life seems to have you stuck in a place of darkness. If this is you, allow me to discuss with you a seldom issue discussed prophetic issue.

Now, my prophetic friend, let us talk about darkness, the friend of the prophet. I promise you that God will use the prophetic arc to expose and prepare you in the darkness.

CHAPTER 11

DARKNESS, THE FRIEND OF THE PROPHET

You feel stuck. Your prophetic arc has landed you here. You feel strange and that God has punished you. You are in a place of darkness and you just don't know why.

Have you ever noticed that things look different in the dark? You see things differently in the light, once you compare them to what you have seen in the dark.

We have grown to associate darkness with evil. Different types of black magic, spells, and evil seem to walk hand in hand. We all need to examine darkness, so we can see its special purpose. God really does have a plan.

As we study human interactions, we look at darkness and pair it up with not knowing. The truth is that darkness is the absence of light. Light is so much more than darkness. Light can be measured, but darkness cannot. Darkness is simply the lack of light.

The seer/prophet needs to understand that darkness is a friend. Darkness in a prophet's life signals that something is absent. This is the signal that something is missing.

When you know you're in the dark, you know there is a void in your life, whether you care to admit it. How many prophets today are hurting because there is an absence, a void in their lives and pride won't let them admit it?

Why do you think that we spend so much of our life here? We are in the dark and can't see, something is missing. Have you ever realized that what is not there in your life, prophet, can be just as painful as what is in your life? We live in a world that spotlights everyone in the light. Have you ever seen prophets as they constantly struggle for the limelight?

The reality is that for a prophet, God does His best work in their life in the darkness. You should thank God that he develops things in you out of so many of your critic's sight. He does it in the darkness. Darkness is a friend prophet that you never knew you had.

When God is ready to elevate or prepare you, He puts you in the dark. Prophet, understand that we are the film of God's plan. We develop in the dark, but we are not developed in the light.

Like film, the stages of our lives as prophets are always developed in a dark room. Understand the prophetic arc and the purpose of the backstory.

So many prophets are seeking the light. We use social media 24/7 for the exposure, but the reality of who we are apart from each other is exposure in the darkness.

This season, those who find themselves in the dark are being prepared for the light in the next season. What we do not have is being prepared within us, as long as we do not try to rush the process. The prophetic arc places us in the place where God works on us.

In *Genesis Chapter 1,* God moved in the darkness of the earth. He called for light from the darkness. He showed us a pattern of how He uses darkness to develop, create, and mature.

Every prophet of God goes through a dark time in a dark place. Did you realize you can find God there? I so wish Jeremiah were here to speak on this topic.

In *Genesis 1:3-5,* God said, *"Let there be light: and there was light."* We see that God spoke and saw it come into fruition. Darkness always moves away from the light. Darkness is the absence of, and it cannot be shared with light. This is the same thing you should consider in your life.

God does much of His absolute best work in the dark. As His prophets, we should imagine what He can do in the dark places in our lives or the places we refuse to let Him in.

Why should we trust God in the dark places of our lives? In *Isaiah 45:33,* God has promised us the treasures of darkness. Our God has hidden riches in secret places not exposed by the light.

God speaks of what He has not shown and will give us. Prophet, eyes have not seen this. Know that the God that we serve is able. He can and will perform His word.

This is God's promise spoken by the Eagle Eye prophet Isaiah. We can trust the promise that God has spoken through His prophet and his work carries a weight that so few of us have ever imagined. Those of you in what you call darkness, rejoice as God has us. We have work to do, prophet.

The prophet is different because of the process God has arranged for us with His tool, the prophetic arc. So many of us grew up looking at darkness. We must learn from the perspective God has us experiencing. Prophet, can we understand that in the dark areas of our lives, God has treasures we never even realized?

God will allow us to go through changes in darkness. As His prophets, we should be thankful that we were not put before people before it was time. We should be thankful that God did not expose certain aspects of our lives. He processed us in the darkness.

Had God allowed some of us to be put in the light before time, the results would have been a disaster. This is why there is such an emphasis on when we will come forth as prophets.

Mentorship is critical and prophets who prefer to move at their own speed soon see the error of their judgement and suffer from a lack of understanding of the purpose of darkness and what it develops in a prophet's life.

Who wants the treasures of darkness as promised by God in *Isaiah 45:3?* Who is ready to claim that promise and come out of your personal darkness? Who is ready to allow God to call light into your life? Those of you in dark places right now need to hear this. You are not being punished. You're being processed.

Your darkness is your privacy that God allows to bring some things out of your life. Generational curses, sickness, jealously, and pride. What does God needs to bring out of your life that has been hidden in the darkness? Could this be where you are at this very moment?

Think about the people you met before God put you in the darkness. Why would I say that? *Romans 8:28* says all things work together for the good of those who love God. All things, including your darkness, are necessary for your development, for the light that you seek to replace the darkness in your life.

God put the first prophet to sleep in the darkness to foster a covenant with him. The great Abraham went into darkness to be in a covenant with God. Notice the covenant is a result of God's work in darkness, affecting generations to come, including today.

Can you understand, prophet, that some of the things you are dealing with now are for your prophetic children and apostolic grandchildren? If you don't allow God to deal with your darkness, then you will be an unwelcome thorn causing darkness in people's lives because you refused to allow God to deal with your darkness.

Think about your children, spiritual children, and future mentees. You got darkness. Darkness is a friend who signals to you that something is missing. There is an absence. This key thing is that unless there is darkness, you will never see the Glory of God.

Prophets so many times, we have been brought up to condemn the darkness in our lives. We curse it in the name of Jesus. We call it not of God, and yet it is the very vehicle God uses to purge us when no one is around.

He will empty and fill us when no one sees it. It's funny how people always see the finished product of the prophet or the semi refined part of our lives as we are on our way to be. They don't see us in the darkness.

Darkness brings an Abraham out of Abram; it brings a resurrected Jesus to light. Darkness is essential to change. *Acts 9: 1-9* says, And Saul yet breathing out threatening slaughters against the disciples.

Saul now journeyed, and as he approached Damascus, he saw a light from Heaven. Saul falls to the ground and hears a voice that changes his life."

He asks, "Who art thou, Lord?" We see the exchange of words as Jesus tells him, "I am whom thou persecute." Notice that he knows who he is speaking to. Can you imagine three days without sight? Saul did not eat or drink.

Look at Saul, a dangerous man, who was sent to darkness. How many of us are like Saul? We are dangerous and represent a generation of hate.

Saul hated people simply because of their belief. He had ideals that were forged throughout his life, and now, as a full-grown man, he has run into a season of darkness.

Prophet, a key point to look at here is that when you hate people because how they believe you are just like Saul, the reality is that you do not know God. You know religion, not a relationship with God that will be fertile for signs, wonders, and miracles in your life.

This is critical for a prophet because they must have a relationship with God or they are in the dark. We are in the dark and in a state of absence like Saul.

Saul, who would become the generational prophet of his time, is on his way to Damascus to kill Christians. He has everything he needs to kill them. He is educated. He has paperwork approved and trained in the art of killing.

Saul has everything he needs to do what he intends to do to the people of God. The Bible says a light shone on Saul and blinded him in his dark life. This is the breaking of an unholy alliance. We see a change in his life. God stopped it.

Prophet, what has God stopped in your life? Was it cancer, Aids, diabetes, gout, Corona virus, poverty, unfruitful relationships, or a bad marriage? Are you like Saul in the darkness and don't know what's happening?

You were almost destroyed, killed, run over, and forgotten, but God stopped it. You're now in the darkness. He is changing you in the process. This is the prophetic arc process in your life and we see it in Saul's/Paul's life.

Saul is blind in the dark and his relationship with God is established. He comes to know Jesus in a way he never knew him before. What was in Saul was an Apostle named Paul. What do we see? We see that Saul was changed in the darkness of his sin. God had a real work for him to do.

Just because you see someone going through something does not mean they did something wrong. It can mean that God has an assignment for that person and in the darkness, He will release His Glory out of that vessel that He has specially placed in position. Someone should shout about that.

Whatever is absence in your life is but for a season because if God has treasures in the darkness, then we must know and accept the fact that He has us there to foster and birth His plan for our next assignment, season, or generation.

Darkness births us and our visions. A seed is planted in a woman's womb to birth a child. The planting is in the dark. You can see and not have a vision. Saul could see the Christians but had no vision.

Darkness now has broken an unholy alliance off his life and birthed a vision within a man who had eyes but no vision. He is birthed within a vision and if you want this type of anointing upon your life, you must understand that darkness is a friend you never knew you had.

A relationship with Christ will allow you to see the vision of who you are and your assigned work. As a small boy, I used to listen to a group called Simon and Garfunkel. They wrote a song called The Sounds of Silence. One verse in particular goes like this:

Hello darkness, my old friend
I've come to talk with you again
Because a vision softly creeping
Left its seeds while I was sleeping
and the vision that was planted in my brain
Still remains within the sound of silence.

This is a vision of a man depending on his own intellect to deal with the missing elements of his life. He is clearly bi-polar and is searching for this insight that only comes from God through a relationship.

In *Acts 9,* Saul changed through the darkness. We will change through our darkness. The key you must understand is that your mentality must be in order or you will be the person that Simon and

Garfunkel sang about, instead of a new creature in Christ. Darkness is your friend, prophet, and now that we know it. Let's turn it over to Jesus and allow Him to do a work within us.

A final point is that too many of us want to plant a seed and see it grow, see the harvest, and see how it changes. The reality is that when a seed is planted, it is just like a farmer planting.

You put the seed in the soil, prayed, and meditated as the farmer tilled the land and pulled the weeds to prepare it for growth. The seed grows down before it grows up. Remember that.

It is a small wonder why prophets have not learned to plant seeds and see the benefit. They do not understand the darkness. The darkness is your friend that you never knew you had, prophet.

Darkness is a vital part of the prophetic arc. Prophet, your backstory is now set. God bless you, prophet. I want to share an important chapter discussing how the prophetic arc moves in and upon your life. This tool of God is awesome, as we can see from the two prophets, Jesus and John The Baptist, who need no introduction.

The prophetic arc will show a prophet who operates in class and has dignity versus a prophetic tramp. Let's talk about this, as it is important.

CHAPTER 12

A PROPHET WITH CLASS VERSUS A PROPHETIC TRAMP

(DEALING WITH THE EGO OF A PROPHET)

Clear understanding is important in the prophetic. The prophet's understanding of where they may be is critical. The prophetic arc will not lie to you or for you either prophet. Understand that it is true to God's intentions and not ours.

So often today, we make false assumptions to fit our personal perspectives. This is the world we live in and the issues it brings to us as prophets.

Mark Chapter 1 highlights my assignment in this chapter. We will look at a prophet with class versus how we identify a prophetic tramp today. Let's dig deeper. We look into verse 1 and see the work of the now generation prophet operating in the Bible days. This is the story of John the Baptist.

Just like you prophet, he is different and unlike his contemporaries. John the Baptist is a new type of preacher, just like many of you to many around you. The prophetic is something they have never been exposed to.

On the other hand, you have never been exposed to people reacting to you this way either. Allow God to use such an opportunity to guide you into what you will see later in life. You know this is happening because your life has shifted this way for a reason.

John the Baptist was a prophet, who preached in the wilderness. He is not concerned about being in a multimillion dollar sanctuary. John the Baptist is where God has placed him. Can you see this is where God has called him? Being different is not a bad thing. It is a necessary thing.

Embrace who you are prophet, even if your peers find you extra funny. Embrace your difference because greatness is connected to being different. God has called you to be different. There is greatness in you that has not come forth yet, but is being prepared. Thank God for the prophetic arc.

Why is all this important? Well, 18 years had passed, and no one had seen Jesus. Now, after 18 years, Jesus showed up in the wilderness in a crowd of people. No one knew who he was.

John the Baptist, the renegade prophet of his day, is preaching about his cousin, Jesus and His return. Can you imagine seeing Jesus in the crowd, whom He has not seen in years and now he has returned?

Picture this, as you read. Everyone is watching John the Baptist, a different type of messenger. He does not fit the status quo. This is what will make or break you. How do you receive those who receive you and those who may not? Are you the same person or do you have an air about yourself? This is a fair question to ask yourself.

As John the Baptist is preaching, imagine ordinary people walking by Jesus to see him preach. They paid no attention to Jesus because they came to see John the Baptist. They know and spend time with him in the wilderness.

Remember 18, years have passed and now John the Baptist is the new hot voice in the pulpit. The people are flocking to see him. He has a word from God in his mouth. They are learning of the God he spoke of.

Now, as the people continued to come, John the Baptist finished and started to baptize them. Again, the people push past Jesus to get to John the Baptist. Read this again. They are walking by Jesus to get to John the Baptist.

The lesson here is that people will often ignore you because your greatness is not yet on full display. Can you see this? The prophetic arc often puts you in this type of position as you go through the process.

They can't see you, so they ignore you. They walk by you to get to who they feel is great at that time. Jesus demonstrates the class need here to demonstrate to us a valuable lesson.

Prophets understand just because time has not exposed your greatness, does not mean that greatness is not in you. Remember you are a work in progress. You're still growing, so being in obscurity, means your still in God's plan! You're being tested so you can be trusted.

Prophet, God will place you to ensure your ego stays in check. Everybody walks by Jesus as He demonstrates the humility that God wants in His prophets. Has God ever allowed people or peers to pass you to keep your ego in the right place? Do you have the capacity to deal with this? Are you the prophet, who presents themselves as a street tramp wanting to be seen?

Yes prophet, people will ignore you with your highly anointed self. They will totally exclude you and God allows it. Look as how Jesus demonstrated this. This is the same Jesus who raised the dead and walked on the water. Can you see yourself walking past him to get to John the Baptist?

While many of you are saying no, again consider the setting. Jesus has been off the scene for 18 years and now he returns to the back of the crowd. No one pays him any attention. Jesus does not attempt to announce himself either.

Let's look at how a prophet with the status of class operates. Class for a prophet is part of the anointing that is caught, not taught. Class for a prophet is a matter of character and integrity.

The class of a prophet displays how that prophet handles themselves. This is how we see Jesus handled himself as He recognized the genuine leadership of John the Baptist.

Jesus is not trying to get attention by holding a prayer line in the back of the crowd, nor do we see Him pulling people to the side because He prophesied to them. He has real prophetic class and demonstrated it.

Jesus is not looking for attention. He is the very opposite of a prophetic tramp. A prophetic tramp is always looking to provide sensationalism. This type of prophet is always inconsistent. They lack responsibility and full of pride.

They get mad when they see a social media post that does not include them. They often try to offset what they see another prophet do. This is one of the main reasons you see them run from church to church or ministry to ministry because of 'the don't you see me?' I am a prophet, don't you see me?

They brag about how they prophesized to this person or that person and how God used them. They see only themselves in a group of people. They have identity problems because of who they feel they are. They are the harlots of the prophetic. Just as we see a harlot walk the street for attention of men or women, and we see it today. The quest is for your attention and to pull you to them for their selfish purposes.

We already know of the physical factor. Let's look at the prophetic spiritually. They are dangerous because they gossip and sow webs of deceit among peer prophets, destroying them in the process.

They are the first cousins of false prophets, as we see them wander back and forth throughout their ministries. They get mad at the drop of a hat and always want to be the victim.

They will walk hand in hand with a Prophet Lot until they fall out with them. They have issues with everyone except themselves because they are always the victim, who wants to be seen and be up front because they are prophets.

Jesus demonstrates that the prophets who hold on to their integrity are always recognized by God when others cast them aside. This is when we see a prophet's character, when God has allowed them to go through the process of being humble, accountable, and consistent. Can you look at his example again?

John the Baptist looks up and sees Jesus. Oh, what a sight to him. He announces Jesus. Behold the lamb of God. How many of you have been announced as prophet, versus how many of us have become prophetic tramps?

Notice that John announces Jesus and sends his attention to him. He knows who Jesus is and takes the attention off him and points it to greatness. How many prophets would do that today? This is also a demonstration of a prophet with class as he speaks, "Behold the lamb of God."

Prophets see that John the Baptist is well-grounded in scripture and demonstrated a deep, abiding relationship with God. His focus is on focus on edification, exhortation, and comfort, as outlined in *1 Corinthians 14:3.* The kingdom principles he demonstrates is so needed today.

Today, we have silent egos that tend to be exposed with our actions. How many times do you fail to recognize a leader because you think it takes away from you? We all see it and so often, we act like it is not an issue. This is a major issue within the prophetic community.

The absolute class John the Baptist shows is how to announce a prophet in a crowd. Jesus went from being unknown to being known. This is class in operation. Look at Jesus. He took 18 years away and now he comes to step in the lime light.

So unlike the prophets of today, who run out because they're mad and were asked to give an offering. They're mad because they did not get to prophesy and get recognized properly. They're mad because there was no room in the pulpit for them. Nobody sees or knows them and it upsets them. Jesus goes through the process of an unknown prophetic ministry and if you walk with God, you will also go through this process.

Prophet, please understand that the prophetic tramp will cause considerable damage and will be responsible for the following and more. People are led astray with false teachings, which creates division within churches. This is the result of the prophetic tramp anointing.

The trail of disillusionment and the aftermath of their ministry often requires extensive healing and restoration work by legitimate spiritual and prophetic leaders.

John the Baptist showed real class as he demonstrated he was about building the Body of Christ. As prophet's outward character should align with biblical standards of holiness, humility, and love.

A prophet with class and a prophetic tramp are different not just in the content of their messages, but in the totality of their ministry and character.

Wisdom and discernment are essential in distinguishing between these two and ensuring that prophetic ministry serves its intended purpose of building up the Body of Christ. The work of the prophetic arc is in full effect and the backstory is established.

ABOUT THE AUTHOR

Apostle Ken Cox started serving God in 1994 after a series of unforeseen life failures. Out of the military and seemly starting life over again, by 2000, Apostle Cox had found his life calling as a Prophet. The challenge of learning and understanding presented a new frontier. Apostle Cox dove into the process and has now emerged as a well-traveled prophet who serves the Body of Christ as an Apostle.

Apostle Cox, along with his wife, Prophetess Sabina Cox are the leaders of Where Eagles Fly Fellowship Inc., a fellowship of prophets and apostle across the USA and beyond who are dedicated and focused on establishing the prophetic gift back into society as they raise up prophets around the country and abroad.

Apostle Cox and Prophetess Cox are available for Revivals, Conferences and Meetings. They have been featured in meetings and sought-after to teach and instruct the prophetic for ministries seeking to learn more about the gift. Apostle and Prophetess Cox have 3 children and 4 grandkids as of this writing and currently reside in Durham, NC. Contact them through the Where Eagles Fly office at 919-695-3375 or 919-213-1328 or at www.whereeaglesfly.us.

He is also the author of the following books:

The Prophet In The Wilderness

Luciferian Spirit Among The Prophets

Meeting The Prophet In My Reflection

Prophet Called to a Cross Culture

Visualization, The Prophet Sees In Adullam

The Prophetic Staff

The Mentality of the Prophetic Staff

The Soul of The Prophet's Health

The Unseen War of the Issachar Seer's Soul

The Soul of the Issachar Seer

A Prophet In The Moment: Understanding Where You Are At In The Prophetic Process

INDEX

errors, 19

essence, 24

evil, 36, 111

example, 5, 9, 14, 17, 34, 53, 56, 58, 79, 124

excuses, 58

exhortation, 125

expense, 8, 39, 45

exposure, 112

eyes, 2, 79, 83, 113, 118

F

Facebook, 39, 48

fact, 8, 17, 22, 26, 27, 28, 33, 35, 38, 44, 46, 47, 48, 66, 67, 69, 71, 75, 84, 88, 91, 100, 102, 108, 109, 118

failures, 16, 127

faith, 11, 31, 32, 52, 58, 61, 62, 70, 72, 75, 86, 87, 88, 89, 94, 95, 96, 97, 105

faithful, 6, 54, 60, 68

family, 2, 25, 28, 43, 52, 55, 94, 95

farmer, 52, 119

fashion, 19, 20

fasting, 19

favor, 11, 20, 45, 46

fears, 31

fellowship, 14, 28, 127

field, 23

film, 112

financial, 25

fitness, 54

flaws, 31

flesh, 47, 61

focus, 22

T

U

www.ingramcontent.com/pod-product-compliance
Lightning Source LLC
Chambersburg PA
CBHW071408120626
46546CB00002B/862